# ☀ INSIGHT COMPACT GUIDE

# ST LUCIA

*Compact Guide: St Lucia* is the ultimate quick-reference guide to this verdant island. It tells you all you need to know about St Lucia's attractions, from its spectacular rainforest to its fine beaches, from towns shaped by pretty squares and French-colonial architecture to colourful underwater treasures around pristine reefs.

This is one of over 133 Compact Guides, combining the interests and enthusiasms of two of the world's best-known information providers: Insight Guides, whose titles have set the standard for visual travel guides since 1970, and Discovery Channel, the world's premier source of non-fiction television programming.

D0111271

**Discovery** CHANNEL

**APA** PUBLICATIONS  L
Part of the Langenscheidt Publishing Group

## Insight Compact Guide: St Lucia

*Written by:* Lesley Gordon
*Edited by:* Pam Barrett and Caroline Radula-Scott
*Photography by:* Richard Nowitz, with additional photography by Anthony
Blake 60; Corbis 80, 91; Jerry Dennis/Apa 88; Lesley Gordon 65/2, 66;
Bob Krist 6, 8/1, 8/2, 10/2, 13, 15, 16, 20–1, 47, 48/2, 52, 54/2, 62/2, 69/2,
71, 73/1, 74, 81, 83, 84, 85/2, 85/3; Nature 17; Rex Features 89/1; courtesy
of the St Lucia Tourist Board 61, 62/2, 68; Terraqua 9, 17/1, 50–1, 67;
Topham 14, 53/2, 82/1, 93; courtesy of Llewellyn Xavier 44, 88
*Cover picture by:* Bob Krist
*Design:* Tanvir Virdee
*Picture Editor:* Hilary Genin
*Maps:* Laura Morris

*Editorial Director:* Brian Bell
*Managing Editor:* Maria Lord

**CONTACTING THE EDITORS:** As every effort is made to provide accurate
information in this publication, we would appreciate it if readers would
call our attention to any errors and omissions by contacting:
*Apa Publications, PO Box 7910, London SE1 1WE, England.*
*Fax: (44 20) 7403 0290*
*e-mail: insight@apaguide.co.uk*

Information has been obtained from sources believed to be reliable,
but its accuracy and completeness, and the opinions based thereon,
are not guaranteed.

© 2004 APA Publications GmbH & Co. Verlag KG Singapore Branch, Singapore.

*First Edition 2004*
*Printed in Singapore by* Insight Print Services (Pte) Ltd
Original edition © Polyglott-Verlag Dr Bolte KG, Munich

Distributed in the UK & Ireland by:
**GeoCenter International Ltd**
The Viables Centre, Harrow Way, Basingstoke,
Hampshire RG22 4BJ
Tel: (44 1256) 817987, Fax: (44 1256) 817-988

Distributed in the United States by:
**Langenscheidt Publishers, Inc.**
46–35 54th Road, Maspeth, NY 11378
Tel: (1 718) 784-0055, Fax: (1 718) 784-0640

Worldwide distribution enquiries:
**APA Publications GmbH & Co. Verlag KG (Singapore Branch)**
38 Joo Koon Road, Singapore 628990
Tel: (65) 6865-1600, Fax: (65) 6861-6438

# www.insightguides.com

# ST LUCIa

## Introduction

## Places

## Culture

## Travel Tips

**△ Diamond Botanical Gardens (p69)**
The tropical gardens are bursting with bright flora such as orchids and coconut trees, called the 'tree of life'.

**△ Anse Chastanet (p67)**
An ideal spot for divers and snorkellers, with a resort and a dive site just metres from the beach.

**◁ Underwater (p66)**
The island has a rich marine life that attracts divers to its pristine coral reefs.

**△ Balenbouche Estate (p77)** The plantation has an 18th-century water wheel and a mill used to process sugar cane.

**◁ Pigeon Island (p40)**
A strategic military post used by French pirates in the 16th century and the US armed forces in the 20th century.

△ **Diamond Falls (p69)**
The beautiful cascades are mineral rich, its waters are believed to be an effective treatment for rheumatism.

△ **Castries (p22)**
The city's colonial architecture has balconies adorned with gingerbread fretwork.

▽ **Sulphur Springs (p71)**
The rocky landscape of this geothermal field contains water that bubbles at very high temperatures.

△ **The Pitons (p75)**
These volcanic cones are spectacular landmarks that feature on everything from T-shirts to tablecloths.

▷ **Grande Anse (p50)**
The endangered leatherback turtle hatchlings rush to the sea from protected nesting sites on the East Coast.

# The Land of the Iguana

Every year, several hundred thousand people visit the tiny island of St Lucia (pronounced *Loo-sha*) which was known as Hewanorra (Land of the Iguana) to the early Amerindians. These visitors often get more than they bargained for from this archetypal Caribbean land of sand, sun and sea.

Most of the year the weather is warm and sunny, tempered by trade winds and light showers. The Caribbean coast has long stretches of fine sand and healthy coral reefs, while the Atlantic-buffeted side provides good windsurfing and has nature reserves populated by rare wildlife. At the island's heart the rich land is lush with trees, and there are pristine rainforests in the mountains and on the Pitons, the landmark twin, cone-shaped peaks. In the valley below farmland punctuates the landscape.

Here too is a colourful Creole culture and the people are, for the most part, open and friendly with a sense of fun and real pride in their homeland. St Lucians are considered to be less cynical and savvy than residents of islands with an older, some might say more jaded, tourism sector, but increasingly they are becoming commercially oriented.

For more than two centuries the land was the subject of bloody battles and a virtual tug-of-war ensued between the acquisitive French and British imperial powers who fought for control. Today, St Lucians still guard their island jealously, and rightly so, because with careful development this tropical paradise, which has a spectacular natural environment, will remain an eco-tourist's dream.

**Windward bound**
The Windward Islands are made up of Dominica, St Lucia, St Vincent and the Grenadines and Grenada.

*Opposite: the spectacular Diamond Falls*
*Below: strolling along Cariblue Beach on the north coast*

## POSITION AND LANDSCAPE

Lying at the southern end of the Lesser Antilles chain, St Lucia is about 2,100 km (1,300 miles) from Florida, with Martinique 34 km (21 miles) to the north, St Vincent to the south and Barbados 160 km (100 miles) to the southeast. The island comprises 617 sq km (238 sq miles) of

*Above: the St Lucia green parrot is known locally as the jacquot*

---

**The Tree of Life**
The coconut palm is known as the 'tree of life' because every part of the tree, from trunk to nut, can be put to good use. The palm leaf is used for roofing, basket-weaving and making hats; the trunk is used in construction, the brown outer fibre and husk of the nut is used in mattresses and pillows, while coconut water, drunk directly from the nut, makes a refreshing drink. Coconut water is also believed to be a good hangover cure.

---

undulating hills and valleys covered with native trees, coconut palms, banana plantations and rainforest that is home to a variety of wildlife such as iguanas, hermit crabs and the national bird, the St Lucia green parrot *(Amazona versicolor)*.

The second-largest of the Windward Islands group – only Dominica is bigger – volcanic St Lucia is 43 km (27 miles) long and 22 km (14 miles) wide, with beaches of black or golden sand, hot sulphur springs, a scenic mountain range and rich, fertile soil. The twin peaks, Gros Piton and Petit Piton, are smaller than the island's highest point, Mount Gimie (950 m/3,118 ft).

The centre of the island is dominated by a mountainous landscape carpeted with lush vegetation. More than 300 m (1,000 ft) above sea level, the cool rainforest covers a large part of the island's interior and southern areas, with a series of stunning waterfalls. Soufrière volcano is dormant – there has been no volcanic activity on the island since 1766 – but vents hydrogen sulphide gases and steam. A tell-tale odour, rather like rotten eggs, sometimes pervades the island's sulphur springs in the Soufrière area, where the rough, rocky landscape is dotted with craters blackened with iron sulphate and pools of bubbling water that reach temperatures of 171°C (340°F). Visitors exploring the Edmund Forest Reserve on foot can take a dip in the breathtaking En Bas Saut waterfall in the south, or sneak away to smaller, lesser-known falls. Bird lovers head to the Fregate Islands Nature Reserve, an offshore sanctuary and breeding ground for frigate birds.

## MARINE LIFE

Lashed by the Atlantic Ocean and bathed by the Caribbean Sea, St Lucia has varied marine life, with protected coral reefs and colourful inhabitants such as angel and parrot fish. It is one of the world's top snorkelling and scuba diving destinations, bringing people back time and again. Whale- and dolphin-watching off the coast can be fun, as can a day spent sport fishing or sailing on a yacht or catamaran, or simply paddling in the warm water.

## CLIMATE AND WHEN TO GO

St Lucia has a tropical, humid climate that provides warm sunshine most of the year, cooled by northeastern trade winds. Showers during the rainy season keep the land lush and green. During the tourist high season (December to April) temperatures can reach 28–31°C (82–88°F) accompanied by a light breeze and the odd, short shower. On the coast and in town the hottest months are June to August, with temperatures averaging 30°C (86°F), while December and January are the coldest, when night and early morning temperatures can drop to 21°C (69°F). The average daily temperature from November to February is 27°C (81°F) and about 22°C (72°F) at night. From April to October daytime temperatures of 23–29°C (73–84°F) are not uncommon. It is several degrees cooler in the rainforest and mountain villages, and colder still in the mountain peaks.

The rainy season runs from June to the end of November and is characterised by sporadic heavy showers. The annual rainfall can be up to three times higher in the mountains and inland (3,450 mm/136 inches) than on the coast (1,500 mm/59 inches), which contributes to the lush forest vegetation and fertile farmland.

The hurricane season is generally between June and October, coinciding with the rainy season. Storms are the most damaging weather

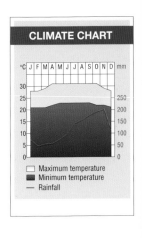

**CLIMATE CHART**

Maximum temperature
Minimum temperature
— Rainfall

*Dolphins are sociable*

phenomena in the Lesser Antilles, but St Lucia's geographical position means that the island is rarely affected by serious disturbances, which is probably why its marinas and sheltered harbours are so popular with the sailing fraternity. However, Tropical Storm Debby, which hit St Lucia in 1994, left several people dead.

## POPULATION

*Below: visitors enjoy water sports on Hummingbird Beach, Soufrière*
*Bottom: schoolchildren in Soufrière*

The island population, which numbers about 160,000, is a pot pourri of people of African, Amerindian, European and East Indian descent. Around 60,000 live in the small area of the capital, Castries, and its environs. In fact, almost 50 percent of the entire population inhabits urban areas. There are more young people than old, which is not uncommon in a developing country, with more than a quarter under 15 years old, almost one-third under 35 and fewer than 10 percent over 65.

Even if their ancestors were born here, it is safe to say that no one in St Lucia is indigenous. European settlement, indentured labour and slavery have helped to determine the ethnic mix of the country. Disease, war and colonisation contributed to the disappearance of the island's Amerindian population, which was virtually wiped out by the time enslaved Africans were introduced in the late

17th-century. Few people can trace their ancestry directly to the early Amerindians, known as Kalinago, as the Caribs can in neighbouring Dominica. However, there are St Lucians who are of mixed African and Amerindian blood.

People with an African heritage are likely to be descendants of the slaves brought as forced labour to work the land, while St Lucians of European heritage are probably the descendants of settlers, plantation owners and poor white labourers. There are also communities of East Indians, descendants of indentured labourers who arrived after the abolition of slavery. Today, around 90.5 percent of the population is of African origin, 3.2 percent of East Indian extraction, 0.8 percent of European origin, with people of mixed heritage making up the remainder. This is a Creole society in its broadest sense: a rich and rare combination of races, cultures, languages and cuisine.

## LANGUAGE AND CULTURE

Although St Lucia has been a British territory since 1814 and the official language is English, French culture pervades. A melodic French Creole (Kwéyòl) is spoken by more than 90 percent of people in informal arenas and, due to a drive to preserve and promote Creole traditions, is increasingly used in official circles as well. It has been suggested that a large percentage of children do not speak English until they go to school. Creole culture and heritage is important and efforts are being made to hold on to the rich folklore, music and language. There are annual festivals, which include traditional storytellers, folk singers and dancers and carnival masqueraders.

The French influence can be seen in place and family names and also in the island's closeness to the neighbouring French *département* of Martinique. There are common linguistic elements within St Lucian and Martinican Creole. However, St Lucian Kwéyòl isn't as close to the French language as one might imagine.

Kwéyòl began as an oral language that initially helped the French and groups from different parts

> ### Weather warning
> A hurricane warning is issued when storm winds reach at least 119 km (74 miles) per hour and high water and storm surges are expected within 24 hours. Warnings should identify specific coastal areas that may be affected by the storm. If ordered to evacuate to a hurricane shelter, follow designated routes as quickly as possible and take only what you will need, such as extra blankets, clothing, medication and a torch.

*The game of warri (also called monkala) was imported from Africa*

of the African continent to communicate effectively. It was derived from elements of French, a variety of African vocabulary and grammar, English and a little Spanish. St Lucian Kwéyòl did not have an official written form until the 20th century and today many people who are fluent Kwéyòl speakers are not literate in the language.

Kwéyòl continues to gain legitimacy through the work of community groups and increasing published literature. In 1998 Kwéyòl was officially recognised in the St Lucia House of Assembly and in 1999 the New Testament was translated into Kwéyòl, a project that took 15 years to complete. Jones Mondesir compiled the first reference and this work was followed by that of Paul Crosbie, David Frank, Emanuel Leon and Peter Samuel, who produced a Kwéyòl dictionary for the Ministry of Education, published in 2001.

## RELIGION

As recently as the 1980s approximately 95 percent of islanders were Roman Catholic but that figure has dropped to around 75 percent due to the rise of evangelical, Pentecostal and other church groups such as Seventh Day Adventists. Anglican membership has remained consistent at about 3 percent. The church plays an important part in the lives of ordinary people, and attending services is as popular in urban areas as in rural villages.

Living by traditional Christian values hasn't prevented St Lucians from retaining elements of the old West African belief system and folklore – *obeah*. An *obeah* man or woman works spells and creates potions from roots and other forest plants that can heal or harm. Before the advent of modern medicine it was the *obeah* practitioner who was sought out to cure illnesses, using ancient herbal remedies. Today, people are turning back to nature in an attempt to recoup knowledge about the medicinal properties of native plants, which flourish in the mountains, jungles and domestic gardens.

*Colonial architecture on Brazil Street, Castries (below) and at Fond Doux (bottom)*

## GOVERNMENT

St Lucia is governed by a multi-party parliamentary democracy based on the British model and led by an elected prime minister. There are two main political parties: the St Lucia Labour Party (SLP) and the United Workers' Party (UWP). A House of Assembly made up of 17 members is elected for a five-year term and the island's Governor General appoints the 11-member Senate.

St Lucia was declared independent on 22 February 1979 but remains a member of the Commonwealth with Queen Elizabeth II as head of state, represented by the Governor General. Immediately following independence the country voted the SLP into office, in effect snubbing the UWP, which had played an important role in the negotiations that helped establish modern St Lucia. John Compton was the leader of the UWP and a pre-independence premier. However, the UWP won the 1982 election and the subsequent two elections, which kept them in power until 1997, when a mixture of domestic problems and disillusionment led to a resounding victory for the SLP. Led by Dr Kenny Anthony, the SLP won 16 of the 17 seats. Not only did Anthony become prime minister, he also held the post of minister of finance. Elections in 2001 returned the SLP to power with 14 of the 17 seats.

The island, which is divided into 11 districts,

> **National symbols**
> Sydney Bagshaw designed the St Lucia coat of arms. The artist Dunstan St Omer designed the National Flag (a royal blue rectangle containing a black, white and a yellow triangle).

*First Communion*

has no army but there is a special paramilitary unit within the police force.

## ECONOMY

The St Lucian economy is based on agriculture. First came the rise of sugar plantations, supported, from the late 17th to mid-19th century, by the slave trade, which provided a workforce to labour in the tropical conditions. After the Emancipation Act of 1834, which came into force four years later, slavery was phased out, but there was little change on the land. St Lucia was never a big sugar producer and by the mid-20th century cheap beet sugar and competition from islands such as Barbados, forced the island to look to other crops, particularly bananas, as a source of income.

*Above: John Compton was premier before Independence in 1979*
*Below: modern Castries*

Over 40 percent of the workforce is involved in agriculture-related jobs, dominated by the banana industry which was once estimated to be worth millions of dollars. The large sugar plantations in the Roseau valley and fertile plains have passed into the hands of individual farmers. Around 80 percent of them work holdings of 2 ha (5 acres) or less, producing bananas for export to the United Kingdom, the main market. St Lucia produces the largest banana crop in the Windward Islands but has been experiencing a slump due to a combination of factors from crop vulnera-

bility to tropical storm damage and competition pushing prices down. In 1997 a World Trade Organisation (WTO) declaration ruled illegal a European Union agreement providing Caribbean banana producers with preferential treatment. The ruling comes into effect in 2006, and the result has been aggressive competition from large, US-backed Latin American producers. (For details see the Caribbean Banana Exporters Association at www.cbea.org)

Overall, agriculture accounts for around 8 percent of the island's gross domestic product (GDP). Another crop that brings in revenue is cassava, and there are continuing attempts by small farmers to diversify, looking to crops such as coconuts.

## TOURISM

The anxiety caused by the end of preferential trade with the EU has been coupled with a decline in manufacturing (which produces some 5 percent of the GDP), especially since the closure in 1999 of foreign plants, which employed hundreds of people. One of the largest of these was Hess Oil, which maintained a large storage and trans-shipment facility outside Castries. These factors made St Lucia look to tourism to keep the economy afloat and there are hopes that restructuring, modernisation and diversification will help.

Contributing 13 percent to St Lucia's GDP, tourism has surpassed agriculture as the island's top foreign exchange earner. More than 30 percent of the workforce is employed in the tourist industry and service sector, from roadside vendors to tour guides, taxi drivers to hotel managers. It is a buoyant sector with more than 260,000 people visiting the tiny island each year, not including the half a million cruise ship passengers.

## FISHING

The St Lucian coast is scattered with small fishing villages where whole communities rely on the fruits of the sea to make a living. Fishing is a tough but financially rewarding business that is very

**The Banana Agreement**
Since the 1950s independent banana farmers in the Caribbean have been guaranteed a market and a stable price by Britain and the EU. The Lomé Convention provided a formal agreement, which covered development aid and price guarantees. But, Latin American banana producers and the US claimed that the trade agreement, which afforded protection and preferential treatment to the Caribbean farmers, was discriminatory. A subsequent World Trade Organisation (WTO) ruling declared the EU agreement unfair and illegal. The small St Lucian growers struggle to compete with the vast plantations in Central and South America producing for US and Latin American companies.

*St Lucia produces the largest banana crop in the Windward Islands*

**Heritage Tourism**
St Lucia promotes heritage tourism aimed at attracting visitors to its natural sites, such as the rainforest and its waterfalls, pristine coral reefs and old estates. The aim is to ensure community participation, cultural preservation, managed development and sustainable tourism.

important to the island's economy; it produced almost 1,800 tonnes of fish in 2000. From Soufrière to Anse La Raye, Laborie and elsewhere, fishermen work in waters that are protected not just from over-fishing but also from the encroaching effects of tourism. Fresh fish such as tuna, dolphin (mahi-mahi or dorado), kingfish, flying fish and snapper caught by local fishermen end up on the menus of St Lucia's restaurants. The island's waters are good fishing grounds for crayfish (spiny lobster) in season; traditional methods using lobster pots and baskets are still used today.

## ENVIRONMENT AND WILDLIFE

St Lucia has a thriving rainforest covering 77 sq km (19,000 acres). Fresh water cascades through the mountains, feeding the rivers and streams in the land below. Protected within a group of nature reserves, including Edmond Forest Reserve and Quilesse Forest Reserve, the dense forest is populated by indigenous and transplanted species such as blue mahoe, introduced from Jamaica, mahogany, bamboo and mango trees and banana and pineapple plants. Bursts of colour come from African tulips, heliconia and hibiscus.

Flora forms the habitat of rare birds and wildlife such as the St Lucia oriole, the red-billed tropic bird and the St Lucia black finch. Nature trails

*A fisherman and seine*

through the forest may also reveal the squirrel-like creature called an agouti, an iguana or a mongoose. Native to the island are the boa constrictor and the deadly fer-de-lance snake, rarely seen because the creatures populate the more dense jungle areas not usually explored by walkers.

Also in the interior are the fertile valleys of Roseau and Cul de Sac where many of the banana plantations are located. In contrast to the lush west, the north of the island is drier, with cacti proliferating in the scrubland.

Learning from the mistakes made during rapid tourism development elsewhere, St Lucia has been mindful to preserve the natural environment that attracts many visitors. Divers and snorkellers flock to the rich and diverse sea life of the coral reefs that border the western and southern areas of the island. The reefs form part of four designated marine reserves that also protect the livelihood of local fishermen.

Along the east coast mainland close to the Fregate Islands are shallow reefs, dry forest and red mangroves. The protected area is a nesting site for the frigate bird, among others.

*Below: the leatherback turtle is a protected species*
*Bottom: a colourful angelfish*

## PRESERVING THE LEATHERBACK TURTLE

The beach at Grande Anse in the northeast of the island is a nesting ground of the leatherback turtle *(Demochelys coriacea)*, the world's largest marine turtle, and an endangered species. During the nesting season the Des Barras Grande Anse Turtle Watch Programme runs guided beach patrols allowing visitors the opportunity to spot the creatures that come ashore to nest.

Leatherbacks nest on the beaches once every two or three years, the only time they leave the sea. During the nesting season (from March to June) the female will lay several times – at least twice, sometimes six times – depositing between 60 and 120 eggs in each batch. There is an incubation period of approximately 60 days. In order to preserve this important cycle it is forbidden to disturb a nesting turtle and remove or damage the eggs or hatchlings.

# HISTORICAL HIGHLIGHTS

**AD 200–400** Amerindians from South America arrive, first the hunter-gatherer Ciboney, then the peaceful Arawak-speaking Taino, whose existence has been dated from shards of pottery unearthed by digs.

**800–1000** The Kalinago, also known as Caribs, arrive; they have a fearsome reputation as warriors because of successfully resisting European attempts at settlement. Amerindians dominate the island they call Hewanorra ('land of the iguana').

**1550s** François Le Clerc is believed to be the first European to settle St Lucia.

**1605** An English ship, *Olive Branch*, lands at Vieux Fort after being blown off course en route to Guiana (Guyana). Of the 67 survivors only 19 are left a month later, they escape in an Amerindian dug-out canoe.

**1627** St Lucia appears in a document for the first time as one of the territories granted to the Earl of Carlisle. There are no immediate attempts to settle the land.

**1635** The French establish a colony in St Lucia, making a counter-claim that the land was granted to M. d'Esnambus by Cardinal Richelieu in 1626.

**1638** Captain Judlee (also known as Major Judge and Jadlee) lands with 300 men. This is the first serious English attempt to colonise St Lucia. The Europeans stay for 18 months and live alongside the Amerindians until a dispute in 1640 leads to many deaths on both sides. The European survivors flee.

**1643** The French appoint a governor to the island, M. Rousselan. Married to an Amerindian, he makes peace and establishes the first permanent settlement.

**1651** The French West India Company claims the island, heralding the arrival of the French.

**1659** The British and the French fight over St Lucia because of its strategic position. The dispute continues for 150 years, during which time the island changes hands 14 times.

**1664** Francis Lord Willoughby, Governor of Barbados, sends 1,000 troops and 600 Amerindians from a base on a neighbouring island to St Lucia. The settlement fails and is abandoned by 1666.

**1666** The French attempt to re-take the island but are thwarted by troops from Lord Willoughby's base on Barbados.

**1667** The Peace of Breda cedes St Lucia to the French.

**1672** Francis Lord Willoughby, Governor of Barbados, St Vincent and Dominica, is appointed governor of St Lucia. The French continue to occupy the island.

**1674** The French West India Company is closed down. St Lucia is annexed to France and established as a dependency of Martinique.

**1686** Another British attempt to take the island is rebuffed by French settlers.

**1722** Treaty of Choc declares St Lucia neutral, calls for the French and British forces and nationals to withdraw until the governments agree on the island's future. However, French, British and Irish settlers who operate estates refuse to leave.

**1744** The Governor-General of Martinique, Marquis de Champigny, sets up a garrison.

**1746** Soufrière is established as the capital under the French.

**1748** St Lucia is again declared neutral in the Treaty of Aix-la-Chapelle. The island remains under French control.

**1762** Admiral George Rodney invades and takes St Lucia, but it is returned to the French under the Treaty of Paris.

**1782** Admiral Rodney destroys the French fleet in the Battle of the Saints off the Windward Islands.

**1789** The French Revolution begins; unrest has implications for the colonies.

**1796** British troops, led by General Sir Ralph Abercrombie, land at Longueville Bay, Choc Bay and Anse La Raye and beat back French resistance taking possession of the island. Fire devastates Castries.

**1802** Treaty of Amiens ends Seven Years' War and returns St Lucia to the French.

**1812** Fire destroys Castries.

**1814** St Lucia is ceded to the British in the Treaty of Paris.

**1838** Following the Act of 1834, slavery is abolished in British territories.

**1842** English is declared the official language of the island.

**1863** Coal is mined commercially in St Lucia for the first time.

**1929** The first airport is built on the island at Castries (called Vigie and later renamed George F. L. Charles Airport).

**1935** Strikes and unrest in St Lucia.

**1951** Universal adult suffrage is established in the British colonies.

**1958–62** St Lucia joins short-lived West Indies Federation; it fails when Jamaica and Trinidad and Tobago break away.

**1964** John Compton, leader of the United Workers Party (UWP), is installed as premier where he stays until independence in 1979.

**1967** St Lucia introduces internal self-government as an Associated State of the United Kingdom.

**1973** Caribbean Community and Common Market (CARICOM) is established.

**1979** The island is granted full independence, while remaining part of the British Commonwealth. The St Lucia Labour Party (SLP) wins the first post-independence election. Sir Arthur Lewis is awarded the Nobel Prize for economics.

**1980** Hurricane Allen strikes the island.

**1992** Castries-born writer Derek Walcott is awarded the Nobel Prize for literature.

**1993** The central square in Castries is renamed Derek Walcott Square.

**1994** Tropical Storm Debby hits St Lucia, 66 cm (26 inches) of rain falls in seven hours. Four people die and 24 are injured.

**1997** Following US and Latin American banana producers' complaints, the World Trade Organisation (WTO) declares the EU-Caribbean special trade agreements unfair and illegal. This has serious consequences for St Lucian banana growers.

**2001** The SLP wins the general election.

**2002** CARICOM announces an agreement to establish a Caribbean Court of Justice.

**2003** Parliament votes to withdraw from Britain's Privy Council.

Map
on page
24

# 1: Castries and Environs

St Lucia's capital, Castries, which lies on the western side of the island, has a population of 60,000. It has been razed and rebuilt four times over the years, leaving few old buildings that have historic or architectural value. But even though much of the town is made up of nondescript modern buildings, Castries still has character and vibrancy. Construction work continues as the city grows.

Visitors who arrive in St Lucia by air will often have their first glimpse of Castries from the road on the drive to their hotel. The lucky ones will enter the city via the Morne on the southern outskirts, looking down over the colourful, sprawling urban area that is Castries and its natural port. At night the view is magical, too, with the town's lights sparkling like thousands of fireflies.

By day, Castries is alive with activity, especially on Saturday when the market is awash with local people doing their weekly shopping and curious tourists enjoying the atmosphere and searching for souvenirs to take home. If there are cruise ships in port, then Castries virtually bulges at the seams.

A tour of Castries can be easily negotiated on foot, as the central area is extremely compact, but a taxi or hire car is recommended when you explore the sights such as Morne Fortune on the southern outskirts.

**Honourable St Lucian**
Born in Castries in 1930, Derek Walcott studied at the University of the West Indies in Jamaica and lived a large portion of his adult life in Trinidad. There he founded the Trinidad Theatre Workshop in 1959. His works include *The Castaway* in 1965, *The Gulf* in 1969, collected Poems 1948–84, the epic *Omeros* in 1990, the play *Odyssey* in 1993 and *Tiepolo's Hound* in 2000.

*Preceding pages: view over Soufrière and the Pitons Below: shopping at the Vendors' Arcade, Castries*

## AN HONOURABLE SQUARE

★★ **Derek Walcott Square ❶** sits at the heart of the capital bordered by Brazil, Laborie, Micoud and Bourbon streets. This quiet square, its well-kept, small green space scattered with a few mature trees, was called Place d'Armes in the 18th century, when it was the site of public executions around the time of the French Revolution. By the late 20th century, the square had undergone two name changes: it was called Columbus Square until 1993, when it was renamed in honour of Castries-born poet and playwright Derek Walcott, who won the Nobel Prize for literature in 1992.

Enter the square either through the west gates on Bourbon Street, facing the beautiful Carnegie Library building, or at Laborie Street, which runs from Jeremie Street at its north end to Brazil Street at the southern end. A tall saman tree (also known as a monkey-pod or rain tree) stands near the east gates on the Laborie Street side of the square; it is believed to be more than 400 years old and offers visitors some shady relief from the tropical sun. A paved pathway runs through the middle of the grassy square linking a memorial obelisk and plaque to the bandstand at the opposite end. The memorial at the west side of the square honours the memory of St Lucians who fought and died in World War I and World War II.

## A JAZZY ATTRACTION

This little square is the site of 'Jazz on the Square', a popular event that attracts visitors and locals who gather here for a daily dose of free music during the St Lucia Jazz Festival, which is held in May. Office workers often use the bandstand and benches here during their lunch hour.

At the centre of the square is a fountain and a little way back towards the bandstand are busts honouring the island's two Nobel Prize winners: Derek Walcott and economist Sir Arthur Lewis *(see page 33)*.

**Star Attraction**
● **Derek Walcott**
**Square**

*Below: Derek Walcott Square*
*Bottom: Carnegie Library*

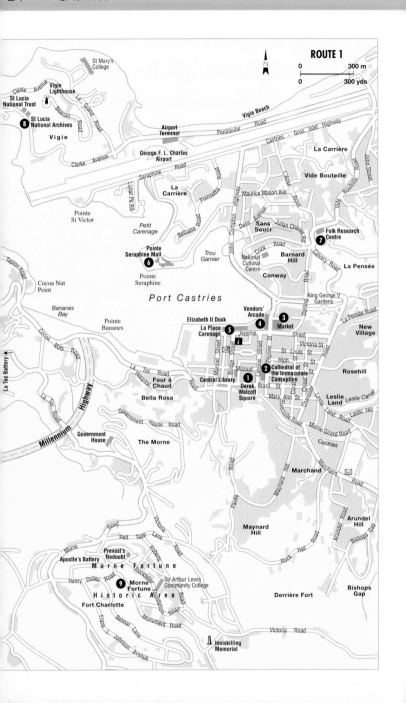

## A Beautiful Cathedral

On the corner of Laborie and Micoud streets is the Roman Catholic cathedral ★★ **The Minor Basilica of the Immaculate Conception ②** (open daily unless Mass is in progress). This has been the site of several churches dating back to the 18th century, but the current building was not completed until 1931. Don't be fooled by the church's shabby exterior; inside there are enough beautiful dark wood pews to seat around 2,000, intricately carved columns and arches, and a stone altar flanked by displays of votive candles, which can also be found near the cathedral's side altars. Yellow light floods the building via decorative windows in the ceiling, which is adorned with a depiction of Catholic saints. Renowned St Lucian artist, Dunstan St Omer, painted the murals on the cathedral walls in 1985 in preparation for a visit by Pope John Paul II the following year. The beautiful paintings reveal the Stations of the Cross with characters inspired by local people. More of the artist's work can be seen in rural churches across the island *(see Jacmel, page 56)* and nearby on Manoel Street there is a mural painted by St Omer and his two sons, who are also artists.

As you leave the cathedral on Laborie Street, to your left is Brazil Street, which has several buildings dating back to the late 19th century.

**Star Attraction**
● Castries Cathedral

*The beautiful interior of the cathedral, the Minor Basilica of the Immaculate Conception*

Map on page 24

Though fading, the wooden structures retain some lovely gingerbread fretwork detail on their balconies. These and the buildings behind were the only ones of their kind to survive Castries' last great fire in 1948.

**A local staple**
Cassava is a root vegetable grown throughout St Lucia. The plant is peeled and grated and the juice extracted, before it is dried to produce farine (a fine flour), which is used to make bread or porridge.

## A BUSTLING MARKET

One of the only other places to escape the flames in 1948 was the old ★★ **Central Market** ❸ situated north of Jeremie Street towards John Compton Highway. Built of iron in 1894, the original market shelter is where you will find the town clock and a modern annexe. Wander through the noisy market where vendors from rural areas sell fresh fish and local produce, including fruit, vegetables, cassava, home-made pepper sauces, spices and basketwork. Across the road on Peynier Street is the ★★ **Vendors' Arcade** ❹, which backs on to the waterfront; you can find an array of souvenirs and gifts including inexpensive, colourful T-shirts, key rings and some very good basketwork, in both traditional and modern styles. Shop around for a good price and don't feel that you have to buy, no matter how persuasive the sales pitch may be.

*Shopping at Point Seraphine*

## SHOP TILL YOU DROP

Heading west from the arcade along Jeremie Street to La Place Carenage, the duty-free shopping mall, the traffic roars past as pedestrians pick their way along the pavement trying to avoid the seemingly endless construction work. The waterfront is on the right-hand side behind buildings that include the district's fire station and central police station. On the opposite side of the road there is a tourist information centre and a small bookshop, which also has a good stock of local newspapers and international magazines.

★ **La Place Carenage** ❺ (Mon to Fri 9am–5pm, Sat 9am–2pm, also Sun if a cruise ship is in town), which lies adjacent to Castries' cruise ship dock, has an entrance on Jeremie Street. The mall has a selection of shops selling crafts and souvenirs, boutiques selling clothing, and art galleries. Across the harbour and reached by a regular water taxi service is the larger and more upscale **Pointe Seraphine** ❻ duty-free shopping mall (Mon to Sat 9am–5pm, also Sun if a cruise ship is in town). This remote but expansive shopping haven is generally quiet during the week because of its distance from the centre of town, but is busier at the weekend and even more so when a cruise ship is anchored at the dock next door. If you don't want to take the inexpensive ferry to cross the water then your best bet is to jump in a taxi for the short drive around the harbour. Travel along John Compton Highway heading north towards George F.L. Charles Airport (formerly known as Vigie Airport), turn left at the fish market complex and continue to the shopping mall. The walk from here to Castries centre isn't that long, but it can seem so, especially in the hot sun.

## EVERYTHING A TOURIST WANTS

Pointe Seraphine has an ATM, a tourist information booth, a kiosk that sells magazines and phone cards, a post box and a Jazz Festival shop and ticket booth. Here, too, are branches of Diamonds International and Colombian Emeralds stores. There are branded goods and quality souvenirs at Bagshaws and Rainbow Trail, while the Clear

**Star Attractions**
● Central Market
● Vendors' Arcade

*Below: waiting for a water taxi in Castries*
*Bottom: a cruise ship dwarfs the dock at Point Seraphine*

Map on page 24

Blue Store is good for locally made ceramics. Trendy boutiques border the pretty courtyard where there are clean toilets and several places to enjoy a drink and a snack. If you want to take advantage of the duty-free prices, remember to take your passport and airline ticket.

## PORT CASTRIES AND VIGIE PENINSULA

The Port of Castries is a busy working harbour where container ships can be seen unloading their contents on to the dock at the North Wharf, adjacent to the Place Carenage duty-free shopping mall. You may see the tall ship, Brig *Unicorn* (tel: 452 8644 for details of tours) tied up at the wharf. The ship, which sets sail from Vigie Cove, is a copy of a 43-m (140-ft), 19th-century brig and operates day and sunset sails with a party atmosphere along the west coast to Soufrière.

The wharf is also the docking place for an inexpensive water taxi that runs every 10 minutes between La Place Carenage and Pointe Seraphine, across the harbour. The L'Express des Iles ferry also operates a regular and fast service to Martinique, Dominica and Guadeloupe from the wharf *(see Practical Information on page 108)*.

The port has two major anchorages at Castries City and another, Vigie Creek, a little further out near the airport. A guide light on Vigie Hill aids

*Above: the military cemetery at Choc Bay*
*Below: the Folk Research Centre, a cultural archive*

the approach to port, but visiting yachts are better off clearing customs at Rodney Bay Marina or Marigot Harbour *(see page 54).*

**Star Attraction**
● **Folk Research Centre**

## CULTURAL ARCHIVE

The ★★★ **Folk Research Centre ❼** (Plas Wichès Foklò; Mon to Fri 9am–4.30pm, tel: 452 2279) stands near L'Anse Road off the Gros Islet Highway, east of the harbour and north of downtown in the hill area of Morne Pleasant. The centre's headquarters is a 19th-century colonial estate house formerly owned by the Deveaux family. Today it houses a cultural archive and a small museum with a reproduction of an indigenous dwelling called a ti-kay hut, some old ceramics, and a variety of traditional musical instruments including a *chak-chak*, named after the sound the seeds inside it make when shaken.

**Sail on the *Unicorn***
The tall ship Brig *Unicorn* *(see page 28)* was used in the filming of the epic television mini-series about slavery, *Roots*. The TV series was based on the book of the same name by the late Alex Haley, which was published in 1976.

On the first floor, the library has an excellent collection of history books, reference material and priceless photographs. This is the island's best folk history resource, which was set up to promote and preserve traditional customs and the Kwéyòl language and art. The centre runs an educational programme in schools and stages tent theatre performances by Teyat Pep La (Popular Theatre), which is also based at the Folk Research Centre. The group performs traditional and modern plays in St Lucian Creole mainly in and around Castries. There are numerous events and performances during La Rose, La Marguerite and Creole festivals and at Christmas, but it is especially busy at Carnival time, when the centre is at its most active.

## MILITARY CEMETERY

Back on Gros Islet Highway head east to the roundabout and take Peninsular Road towards the airport, a small landing strip for Caribbean inter-island and domestic flights. As you round the corner to join Peninsular Road, with the airport runway on your left, you will see the raised white tombstones and monuments in the small military cemetery created for the men of the West India

*The candle-like flowers of pachystachys* (pachystachys lutea) *are a familiar sight*

Map on page 24

*Below: Government House*
*Bottom: ubiquitous hibiscus*

Regiment. South of the runway is a complex that houses government offices and the Pointe Seraphine shopping mall, while the public Vigie Beach runs alongside the road on the right. Though the water here is calm the beach isn't as well kept as others further up the coast, but there are a few benches for picnickers.

## A MILITARY STRONGHOLD

Continue west along the Vigie Peninsula heading up the steep hill towards the St Lucia National Trust and the St Lucia National Archives, which are housed in restored 19th-century military buildings with small verandas. The entire peninsula was once a military stronghold and the barracks and other buildings have been restored.

The **St Lucia National Archives** ❽ (Mon to Fri 8.30am–4.30pm; tel: 452 1654) is a valuable historical resource containing photographs, books, newspapers and journals, many stored on microfilm. Take a pencil (pens are not allowed) to make notes. There is also a photocopying service, for a fee. Next door is the headquarters of the **St Lucia National Trust** (Mon to Fri 8.30am–4.30pm; tel: 453 7656). The trust was established in 1975 as the result of a campaign to save the Pigeon Island Landmark *(see page 40)* from being used for a housing development. Its aim is to preserve the natural and cultural heritage of St Lucia, including areas of outstanding natural beauty, and bio-diverse and historic sites such as Pigeon Island, Fregate Island and Maria Islands. Tours and visits to National Trust properties can be arranged through the Castries office

## BEACON

**Vigie Lighthouse** stands at the end of Beacon Road on the peninsula, on the northern side of the city harbour. The light from the red lantern at the top of the 11-m (36-ft) white tower, built in 1914, can be seen about 50 km (30 miles) out to sea. The lighthouse overlooks military barracks, 18th-century ruins and other historic buildings managed by the National Trust. From here on a clear day there are spectacular views of the southern, northern coasts and Martinique.

In another restored military barracks, north of the lighthouse and close to the top of Le Grand Road before you reach the radio mast, is St Mary's College Catholic boys' school.

## ON THE MORNE

The historic Morne area around Fort Charlotte is accessible from the southern end of downtown Castries. Head west out of town along La Toc Road, with the harbour on the right-hand side, and up the hill in the direction of the Millennium Highway. Before you reach the historic district you will see **La Toc Battery** (tours by appointment; tel: 452 6039), a fine example of a 19th-century battlement. Built by the British, La Toc has cannons, underground tunnels and munitions storage rooms where valuable artefacts are on display. The 1-ha (2½-acre) site has good views of the capital and there is a pretty garden, through which you are free to wander, with or without a guide. Also at La Toc is a luxury, all-inclusive hotel.

Just a few minutes from the battery on the hill is the studio of **Bagshaws of St Lucia** (tours by appointment; tel: 452 6039). The factory uses traditional silk-screen methods to produce

> **Workers' champion**
> George Frederick Lawrence Charles was St Lucia's first Minister of Education and Social Affairs and first Chief Minister. He came to prominence in 1945 when he championed the cause of striking construction workers who were employed to build an extension to the airport. Charles later became the secretary of the St Lucia Workers Co-operative Union. Knighted in 1998 for his contribution to public service, the international airport in Castries was renamed in his honour and a sculpture of the trade unionist was erected there in 2002.

*A cannon at the ready at Fort Charlotte*

Map on page 24

### The Brigands

In 1794, the new French Republic granted freedom to enslaved Africans in its foreign territories. But when St Lucia was again brought under British influence the newly emancipated islanders, fearing they would be returned to bondage, banded together, joined by a number of French army deserters, to create l'Armée Française dans les Bois. The rebels – called Brigands by their enemies – led a campaign of resistance across the island. In 1795 they took control of the fortifications at Pigeon Island, but victory was short-lived. In 1796 British forces defeated and captured them at Morne Fortune.

colourful prints on fabric, with motifs inspired by island flora and fauna, such as hibiscus, parrots and butterflies. The organised tours are worth taking. The company has shopping outlets all over the island, including at La Carenage and Pointe Seraphine in Castries and at Hewanorra Airport.

Travelling further up the hill, you could take a detour to Government House Road, which branches off to the left and leads to **Government House**, the official residence of the island's Governor General. Built in 1895, the colonial building is not open to the public.

## HISTORIC MORNE FORTUNE

Back on the main road, continue up to the 29-ha (72-acre) ★★★ **Morne Fortune Historic Area** ➒ on top of the hill, where you will find the old military buildings of **Fort Charlotte**. The French began building the original fortress in 1768, choosing 260-m (850-ft) Morne Fortune because of its unmatched vantage point of the harbour. When they took control of St Lucia in 1814, the British continued the work and strengthened the fortifications. It was they who named it Fort Charlotte. The fort remained an important defensive base until early in the 20th century. The military barracks and other buildings have been restored and converted to government offices and also

*A woodcarver displays his work*

house the Sir Arthur Lewis Community College, named after the island's first Nobel Prize winner, who is buried here. Nearby are the ruins of Apostle's Battery, with a large mounted cannon, built in 1890 to support the fortress; and the lookout point at Prevost's Redoubt, a French construction dating from 1782.

At the southern boundaries of the fort complex is the **Royal Inniskilling Fusiliers Memorial**, a monument to the soldiers who battled for this position against the Brigands *(see margin box)* and the French in 1796. The monument also marks one of the best viewpoints on the Morne, affording stunning coastal views to Pigeon Island in the north and as far as the Pitons on the west coast.

## AN ARTISTIC COMMUNITY

The hills around Morne Fortune are dotted with hotels and restaurants. Here, too, is a small artistic community that includes the Goodlands workshop of the St Lucian sculptor and woodcarver Vincent Joseph Eudovic *(see page 93)*. At the ★★ **Eudovic Art Studio** (Mon to Fri 7.30am–4.30pm, Sat and Sun until 3pm; tel: 452 2747) woodcarvers produce smooth abstract carvings. The works are made from the ancient roots and stumps of the laurier canelle, and also from laurier mabouey, teak, mahogany and red and white cedar. The Eudovics also have a guesthouse and restaurant on the property.

*Art from indigenous wood at Eudovic Art Studio*

The home of ★★ **Caribelle Batik** (Mon to Fri 8am–4pm, Sat 8am–noon, Sun if a cruise ship is in port; tel: 452 3785), Howelton House is a fine example of Victorian architecture with a Caribbean twist. The pretty building on Old Victoria Road has been carefully restored and houses a batik studio and print shop, which uses Indonesian techniques to create vibrant designs on British and sea-island cotton. The fabric, printed with images of St Lucia's flora and fauna, such as colourful heliconia, is then made into clothing, wall hangings and souvenirs that are sold in Caribelle's shop. Visitors can enjoy light refreshments on the patio where there are views over Castries and its port.

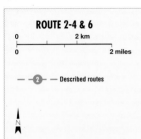

## ROUTE 2-4 & 6

0        2 km
0                    2 miles

— ②  — Described routes

N

CARIBBEAN

SEA

Labrellotte
*Labrellotte*
Masson

**Rat Island**

D'Estrées Point
**George F. L. Charles Airport** ✈
Port Castries
②
④
**Castries**
③

Coubaril Point

Ciceron Point
*Grande
Cul de Sac
Bay*     ○Ciceron
Bananes Point

Morne ○ Soucis
St Joseph
La Croix
Maingot
Marigot Point              Marigot ○
*Marigot Harbour*                      Barre
Marigot Bay                          Duchaussee
**Roseau Valley**
**Banana Plantation** ★
③
*Roseau Bay*  ○**Roseau**     ○Jacmel
Massacre **Distillery**
**Roseau Valley**
**Banana Plantation** ★
Vanard ○

Anse La Raye
*Anse Galet*     ★ **La Sikwi**
Pointe la Ville   **Sugar Mill**

*Anse Cochon*            Durandeau
*Grande Rivière de L'Anse La Raye*

*Anse La Voutte*
Jambette Point        ④
**Plas Kassav** ★  Anse
La Verdure               Roseau
Canaries ○

*Anse La Liberté*        *Canaries*   **Grand Bois**   Millet
**Soufrière** ◄              **Forest**

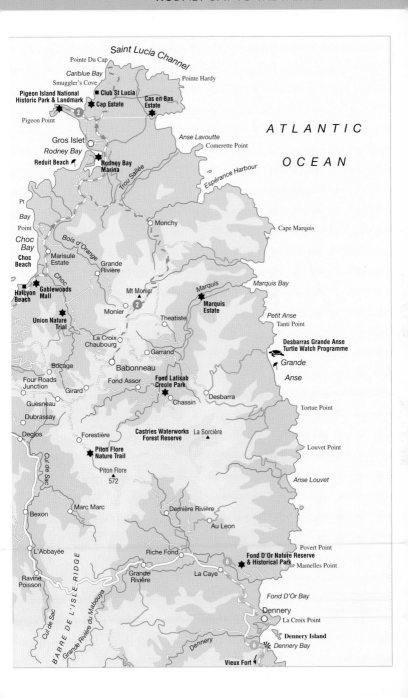

Saint Lucia Channel

Pointe Du Cap
Cariblue Bay
Smuggler's Cove
Pointe Hardy

Pigeon Island National
Historic Park & Landmark
■ Club St Lucia
★ Cap Estate
Cas en Bas
Estate

Pigeon Point

ATLANTIC

OCEAN

Gros Islet
Rodney Bay
Anse Lavoutte
Comerette Point

Reduit Beach
Rodney Bay
Marina

Trou Sallée
Espérance Harbour

Pt
Bay
Point

Monchy
Cape Marquis

Choc
Bay

Bois d'Orange

Choc
Beach

Marisule
Estate

Grande
Rivière

Mt Monier
Marquis
Marquis Bay

Marquis
Estate

Halcyon
Beach
■ Gablewoods
Mall

Choc

Petit Anse
Tanti Point

Union Nature
Trail

Monier

Theatiste

Desbarras Grande Anse
Turtle Watch Programme

La Croix
Chaubourg

Garrand

Grande

Bocage

Babonneau

Anse

Four Roads
Junction

Fond Assor

Fond Latisab
Creole Park

Girard

Chassin
Desbarra

Guesneau

Tortue Point

Dubrassay

Deglos

Castries Waterworks
Forest Reserve

La Sorcière

Louvet Point

Forestière

Cul de Sac

Piton Flore
Nature Trail

Piton Flore
572

Anse Louvet

Marc Marc

Dernière Rivière

Bexon

Au Leon

L'Abbayée

BARRE DE L'ISLE RIDGE

Riche Fond

Povert Point

Fond D'Or Nature Reserve
& Historical Park

Mamelles Point

Ravine
Poisson

Grande
Rivière

La Caye

Cul de Sac

Grande Rivière du Mabouya

Fond D'Or Bay

Dennery

Dennery
La Croix Point

Dennery Island
Dennery Bay

Vieux Fort

Map on pages 34–5

**Rodney Bay**
Rodney Bay is named after Admiral George Brydges Rodney, who claimed St Lucia for the British in 1762 and later established a naval base at nearby Pigeon Island.

# 2: Rodney Bay and the Far North

**Castries – Rodney Bay – Reduit Beach – Gros Islet – Pigeon Island National Historic Park – Pointe de Cap – Babonneau – Grande Anse**

The coastal region to the north of Castries is the island's foremost resort area with sheltered bays, upmarket hotels, quaint fishing communities, a marina, shopping malls and historic landmarks. In the northeast turtles nest, while rural life inland continues much as it has for generations.

From Castries head north on John Compton Highway passing the government offices on the right-hand side, with the port on the left. At the end of the highway turn on to the Castries–Gros Islet Highway, which parallels Peninsular Road leading to the airport. At the roundabout take the second exit for Rodney Bay. The St Lucia Tourist Board administrative office is located in a building close to the roundabout to the right of the highway. The journey north to the Rodney Bay resort area and beyond from the capital is straightforward. Bus No. 1A follows a route to Gros Islet from the Castries bus terminus behind Central Market. The roads along this coast are good, if a little winding, so driving a hire car is hindered only by the lack of signage, although this is much better than in some rural areas.

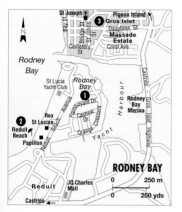

## US-STYLE SHOPPING

The highway is flanked by tree-shaded properties, including Sandals Halcyon Beach, one of the hotel chain's three all-inclusive resorts on this coast. Almost opposite the resort entrance, about 3km (2 miles) from Castries, is **Gablewoods Mall** a large, American-style, indoor shopping area clearly visible from the road. This modern precinct in Sunny Acres includes a supermarket, boutiques and clothing outlets, a pharmacy, gift shops and a large branch of the island's own Sunshine Bookshop (tel: 452 3419). There is plenty of parking here too.

## CALM WATERS

West of the highway, several more hotels and restaurants nestle in the curve of **Choc Bay** and along Choc Beach, which is lapped by the calm waters of the Caribbean. Continuing north, the highway passes above the River Choc and the road winds on through the Quarter of Gros Islet and its undulating hills. To the west, in Bois d'Orange, several hotels are scattered around the hill overlooking **Labrellotte Bay**. From here there are splendid views along the coast and over the bay, which has two good diving sites: Labrellotte Point and Masson Point.

Off the highway, the roads in rural St Lucia lack signposts and can be severely potholed and difficult to negotiate, even in a four-wheel drive, which is why organised tours are a popular option for many visitors. However, it is possible to go it alone, especially around the main tourist centres of Castries, Rodney Bay and Gros Islet.

## ON THE BEACH

The Castries–Gros Islet Highway continues north. Keep an eye out for J.Q. Charles (J.Q.'s) supermarket at Rodney Bay Mall on the left-hand side of the road, at ★★ **Rodney Bay ❶**, a former US military base. Taking a left turn at the mall will lead you to Reduit Beach Avenue, where there

**Star Attraction**
● **Rodney Bay**

*Below: J.Q.'s at the mall*
*Bottom: children play in the waves at Choc Beach*

Map on pages 34–5

is a bank with an ATM, several lively bars, restaurants and small hotels. Also on this road is the **Rex St Lucian and Papillon** hotel complex, which is backed by ★★★**Reduit Beach ❷**, one of the best stretches of sand on the island. The crescent-shaped beach extends as far as Pigeon Island *(see page 40)* further north, interrupted only by the yacht harbour and marina. There is public access to the beach, where visitors can rent sun loungers and umbrellas, indulge in water sports by hiring equipment from a vendor working out of the Rex St Lucian hotel, or simply enjoy a paddle in the clear waters. In high season, when the hotels are full, and at weekends, when local people visit the beach, it can become crowded, but there is usually space enough for everyone to have fun in the sun, but if you are looking for tranquillity, come on a weekday in the off season. Vendors work this beach, but if you are not interested in what they have to sell a polite 'no thank you' is usually all it takes to discourage them.

## CUISINE AND CULTURE

Less than a 10-minute walk from the sand, back on Reduit Beach Avenue, there is a choice of bars and restaurants good for a drink, a light snack or a substantial meal. There is something for everyone from pizza to Thai, continental and

*Below: west coast beaches are good for water sports*
*Bottom: the sheltered marina at Rodney Bay is popular*

American to Caribbean. Worth visiting is The Lime, a casual restaurant and bar serving reasonably priced, hearty local dishes and snacks. The Italian fare at Capone's and La Piazza is good, and Shamrocks Pub, a late-night spot that is best at weekends, is also popular. The **Teyat Pep La** (Popular Theatre) stages a variety of tent-theatre performances in English and Kwéyòl on a site near the satellite police station off the avenue. Access to the tent is via the road that runs behind it, almost parallel to the avenue. Facing on to the road is a notice board that details the theatre schedule; for information about tickets and performance, contact the Plas Wichès Foklò (Folk Research Centre; tel: 452 2279).

## SAILORS' CHOICE

If you are staying in the bay area, Rodney Bay Mall offers more choice than the hotel shops. The mall has boutiques and shops selling gifts, books and newspapers, as well as J.Q.'s supermarket and an off licence. Further along the highway, past the **Bay Gardens Hotel**, there is a large supermarket and a cinema showing the latest movies imported from the US.

★★ **Rodney Bay Marina** and its harbour were created less than half a century ago by an ambitious programme that reclaimed a mangrove swamp. The popular marina is well equipped and is considered to be among the Caribbean's best, with good shops, places to eat and drink, and bank facilities. The bars and restaurants in the area, and around the marina in particular, host lots of activities that revolve around the **Atlantic Rally for Cruisers** (ARC), a big winter event on the sailing calendar. Yachts from all over the world take part in this annual transatlantic rally, setting sail in November from Las Palmas in Gran Canaria to Rodney Bay in St Lucia. The 2,700-nautical mile journey takes anything from 12 to 24 days, and festivities around the marina continue as long as it takes for the vessels to reach their destination.

★★ **Gros Islet** ❸ (pronounced *grows ee-lay*), just north of the marina, is a small, typical fishing

★

**Star Attractions**
● **Reduit Beach**
● **Rodney Bay Marina**

*Below: dancing at Gros Islet
Bottom: there are plenty of
places to dine in Rodney Bay*

Map
on pages
34–5

**The Atlantic Rally**

The Atlantic Rally for Cruisers is the largest trans-ocean sailing event in the world. It was established in 1986 as a fun race for yachts and crews making their annual winter voyage from the Mediterranean to the Caribbean. Hundreds of vessels sail together across the Atlantic Ocean from the Canary Islands to Rodney Bay Marina in St Lucia, which has been the rally's finishing point since 1990.

*Partying at the Friday Night Jump-up*

village that during the week is an antidote to the pace of the busy harbour. However, the hamlet comes alive for a street party on Friday evening.

Single- and two-storey wooden buildings line the streets and while some retain a little faded character most are unimpressive. Most notable is **St Joseph the Worker Roman Catholic Church** at the north end of Bridge Street, on Church Street. It was built in 1926 on the site of an earlier church that was destroyed in the devastating earthquake of 1906. At the end of Dauphine Street, the main road, is Bay Street and a small strip of sand where you are likely to see few people save a handful of fishermen working on their boats and nets. It is safe to swim here but there are much better beaches close by, such as Reduit Beach *(see page 38)* south across the harbour and the Causeway Beach at Pigeon Island National Landmark *(see below)*.

## FRIDAY NIGHT JUMP-UP

Most visitors come to Gros Islet for the **Friday Night Jump-up**, a popular street party when tourists and locals converge on the area. Food and snack vendors line the usually quiet streets, bars and restaurants fling open their doors and sound systems flood the air with the beat of reggae, calypso and soca. This is a good place to enjoy some tasty St Lucian dishes, such as a locally caught fried fish, chicken or conch, then work off the calories by dancing the night away in the crowded street. Things don't hot up until after 10pm and festivities go on in to the wee hours. This is a friendly, fun event with a carnival atmosphere as long as you use your common sense: keep your wits about you and always travel in a group. Generally it is pretty safe, with police, uniformed and plain clothed, on duty.

## HISTORY OF A NATIONAL LANDMARK

Around the bay from Gros Islet, north on the Gros Islet–Castries Highway, head northwest to ★ ★ ★ **Pigeon Island National Landmark** (daily 9am–5pm; interpretative centre closed on Sun;

entrance fee). This was once a separate island, accessible only by boat, but was joined to the mainland by a man-made causeway, completed in 1972. The causeway encompasses a large Sandals all-inclusive resort and a good beach that stretches around the bay to the jetty in the park and offers some interesting offshore snorkelling opportunities. The resort has claimed part of the sand for its guests and more still is sectioned off within the park area, but there is still a good part of it open to everyone. Just before the entrance there is a small parking area and you can buy souvenirs or a snack from the vendors who trade close to the public access point to the beach, which is popular with local people.

Owned and operated by the St Lucia National Trust, Pigeon Island is of significant archaeological and historical importance. It is also the venue for concerts and other events, including the annual St Lucia Jazz Festival. The hilly land that spans 18 ha (45 acres) is thought to have been inhabited by Amerindians, who used the island's caves for shelter and grew staple crops such as sweet potatoes and cassava (manioc). Later the site played its part during the 18th- and 19th-century squabbles between European imperialist powers over control of St Lucia. The island's strategic position and usefulness as a lookout made it a popular choice as a military base. French

**Star Attractions**
● Pigeon Island
● Gros Islet Jump-up

*Above: a Gros Islet cook-up*
*Below: the crescent-shaped beach at Pigeon Island*

Map on pages 34–5

WELCOME TO
PIGEON ISLAND
NATIONAL
LANDMARK

pirates used the island in the 1550s and Admiral Rodney established it as a naval outpost in 1780. He sailed from here to defeat the French forces two years later at the Battle of the Saints, which took place off the Iles des Saintes between Guadeloupe and Dominica. The Brigands *(see page 32)* captured the island in 1795, forcing the British to abandon St Lucia for a while.

By the early 20th century, Pigeon Island was leased to Napoleon Olivierre from St Vincent, who operated a whaling station. Later, in 1937, land was leased to Josset Agnes Hutchinson, an actress with the D'Oyly Carte Opera company. There was a hiatus during World War II when the US established a communications station and a naval air station here. In 1947 Hutchinson returned to her house in the south of the island (now a ruin), opening a beachfront restaurant, which attracted a colourful yachting crowd. She finally gave up the lease in 1970 and returned home to Britain in 1976, dying a year later.

## AROUND THE PARK

Passing through the gates of the park you will be faced with a useful map of the area. The path to the right leads to the ruins of the **Officers' Kitchen** and a little further up the hill is the renovated

*The ruins of Fort Rodney, Pigeon Island*

**Officers' Mess**, a lovely building with a veranda, which houses the small **Interpretative Centre** and shop. Artefacts and historical displays explain the history of Pigeon Island. Below the centre is **The Captain's Cellar Pub**, which remains open after the park closes at 5pm. Wedding ceremonies are held in the white gazebo that stands on an expanse of grass to the left of the path leading to the Officers' Mess and back towards the park gates.

In late spring the property is a popular venue for the St Lucia Jazz Festival *(see page 93)*. The stage is usually set up near the Officers' Mess, using the ocean as a beautiful backdrop, and crowds arrive early to find a good spot on the grass from which to enjoy the show.

## ANIMAL, MINERAL AND VEGETABLE

You can take a guided tour around the park or simply wander along the paths and trails at leisure. There is a variety of flora, fauna and many old buildings, some no more than a collection of stones, others that have survived the ravages of time. The old **Cooperage** has been transformed into public toilet facilities, while an overgrown **military cemetery** holds the graves of old soldiers and sometimes their families, too. On the waterfront, just before you reach the cemetery, is the Jambe de Bois restaurant, a good choice for a drink, an ice cream or a snack. There is a jetty and ferry dock nearby and the lovely beach leads back almost level with the park border and entrance.

## LOOKOUT POINT

On a hill, at the southwestern tip of the park, are the ruins of **Fort Rodney**, which had an excellent vantage point. Today, the fort ruins still afford a good view south towards Castries, but the best lookout point is at 110-m (361-ft) **Signal Peak**. It's a bit of a climb to reach the peak, especially in the hot sun, but it's worth it for the view over neighbouring Gros Islet and far north to Martinique. There is another lookout at the **Two-Gun Battery** close to the **Soldiers' Barracks**.

**Star Attraction**
● Pigeon Island
Interpretative Centre

**Whaling**
Napoleon Olivierre, a native of St Vincent and head of a family with a tradition of whaling, was granted permission to establish a whaling station on Pigeon Island in 1909. In the 1920s a small fleet of schooners operated from the bay area around the island, setting up a winch to haul in a whale on the rare occasions that one was caught. Here too were facilities to extract the precious, but foul-smelling, oil from the creatures. Government legislation effectively ended whaling on Pigeon Island in 1926.

*The renovated Officers' Mess*

Map
on pages
34–5

**Pigeon Island**
Some of the trails around the 18-ha (45-acre) Pigeon Island National Landmark park are coloured with the blossom of bright red flamboyant, Brazilian oak, palm trees and cactus.

## OFF THE BEATEN TRACK

Visitors to St Lucia's far north will find resorts away from the well-trodden tourist track and a viewing point with panoramic views over the St Lucia Channel and Martinique.

**Cap Estate** lies in once-fertile land that was heavily forested. Crops such as tobacco thrived here before the sugar boom of the 18th and 19th centuries resulted in the land being cleared to plant sugar cane. The properties that sit on the former 607-ha (1,500-acre) plantation today are not farmhouses but the exclusive homes of the wealthy. Beyond them lie two all-inclusive resorts, with the prerequisite 18-hole golf course.

## MULTI-MEDIA ARTIST

*Llewellyn Xavier's art is rich and colourful*

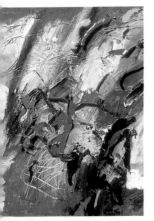

In a mansion house on the estate is **Llewellyn Xavier's Studio** (tel: 450 9155), where the work of the St Lucian multi-media artist can be viewed only by appointment. His art is exhibited in the permanent collections of museums and galleries all over the world including the Smithsonian Institution in Washington, the Metropolitan Museum of Art and the Museum of Art in New York and the National Gallery in Jamaica. Xavier's art can also be seen at Saint Lucia Fine Art, his gallery in Pointe Seraphine *(see page 27)*. The artist's use of oils, watercolours and mixed media reflect the vibrant colours and rich textures of the Caribbean. His first major work in the 1970s was a series of 25 prints dedicated to George Jackson, a young man whose incarceration in America became an international cause célèbre. The prints formed part of a worldwide protest against Jackson's imprisonment. Xavier continues to speak out on social and, more recently, environmental issues, both at home and abroad.

## LARGE HOTELS

Past the luxury homes that pepper the Cap Estate and at the end of a tree-shaded drive, is Great House Restaurant, which is built on the foundations of the estate's original plantation house.

The remote bay and the beach around ★★**Anse Bécune** is dominated by large hotels, but there is public access to the lovely white sand. Visitors not staying at Club St Lucia can buy a day pass that allows use of the hotel's water sports, changing rooms, toilets and other facilities. If you would prefer not to pay a fee to get to the beach through the resort there is a path that leads directly to the sand south of the hotel.

There is excellent snorkelling to be had at ★★**Smuggler's Cove** a little further north. With a sheltered beach and a rugged cliff landscape it is often a little quieter than the neighbouring beach. Public access is down a set of steps beyond the luxury Le Sport resort. Club St Lucia maintains a beach bar here but it is only open to hotel guests so remember to pack your own snacks and drinks. A small inn, the Hotel Capri, is an antidote to the large resorts that dominate this remote part of the island. Housed in an old colonial-style building that was once an embassy, the Capri has stunning views overlooking **Cariblue Bay**.

## THE FAR NORTH

At the far north tip of St Lucia, less than 500 m (550 yards), or about 10 minutes' walk, from Smuggler's Cove is **Pointe du Cap**. At a little under 150 m (470ft) high, in a hilly region beyond

**Star Attractions**
● Anse Bécune
● Smuggler's Cove

*Fun in the sea and on the beach at Cariblue Bay*

**Map on pages 34–5**

**Crayfish**
A traditional crayfish pot is made of strips of bamboo lashed together, forming a tube that is laid on the river bed. One end is sealed up while the other has a flap to allow access to the creatures caught in the pot. Bait can include fresh coconut, which is used at Fond Latisab Creole Park *(see page 48)*.

the Saline Point residential development, Pointe du Cap provides panoramic views across the north coast to Martinique, west to the Caribbean Sea and east to the Atlantic Ocean. If you choose to explore the area without a local guide remember that the roads off the highway in the north aren't always in good condition and at times can be impassable in anything but a four-wheel drive – sometimes not even then. Check the status of the roads before setting off and if you make it, the view at the end of the route will be well worth it. The sea below the sheer cliffs is rough and the land is dry scrub with cacti a common sight. You can't drive to the lookout point so park below and walk up. To the east is Pointe Hardy where paths for walkers criss-cross the undulating land. The area is slated for development and preservation by the St Lucia National Trust, but as yet no work has begun.

## A COLLECTION OF QUIET BEACHES

South of Pointe Hardy on the northeast Atlantic side of the island is ★★**Cas-en-Bas**, known for its collection of quiet beaches. There are no lifeguards, not all the beaches are well maintained and the roads leading to this coast are rough and hard to negotiate, but they are ideal if you want a quiet day away from it all. You can employ a

*View of Le Sport resort at Cariblue Bay*

local guide to travel with you in a small group or, if you are feeling energetic, you could make the journey from Gros Islet on foot in around an hour – it has been known.

Leaving Gros Islet on Dauphine Street, take the road across the highway towards Cas-en-Bas. The beaches are in a sheltered and rocky bay and although the Atlantic waters can be rough the swimming and snorkelling are usually good here. Further south still is **Anse Lavoutte** and a beach where leatherback turtles have been known to nest. Turtle-watch and beach patrols here and at Grande Anse on the east coast are organised by the Des Barras Sea Turtle Watch Group *(see page 51)*.

## TO THE INTERIOR

From the far north return back along the way you came following the route south towards Rodney Bay and the nation's capital. East of Castries and the resort strip is the north's picturesque rural interior that stretches across to the rugged Atlantic coast. The area is rarely visited by the average tourist, but visitors who want to get closer to St Lucian country life will not be disappointed. The land is largely given over to agriculture and small village communities barely affected by tourism development elsewhere.

Travelling from Castries this eastern detour will take you off the Castries–Gros Islet Highway north of Choc Bay and the Bois d'Orange district. The Allan Bousquet Highway leads to the village of Monchy and St Lucia's rural interior: Babonneau, Fond Assau and Des Barras. There are a few basic bed and breakfast places off the beaten track here, which are inexpensive and homely but are only practical if you have transport because taxi fares will mount up if you want to do an excursion every day. South of Monchy, through winding roads, is **Babonneau** in the heart of farmland and plantations. The area around Babonneau and Fond Assau is thought to be the place to which the last group of African-born enslaved people were transported, which probably accounts for the strong African tradition that has been retained.

**Star Attraction**
● Cas-en-Bas

*Below: fragrant frangipani (Plumeria rubra)*
*Bottom: the snorkelling is good in Atlantic waters*

Map on pages 34-5

Below: cocoa pods on a tree
Bottom: from coconut to copra

## PRESERVING THE PAST IN THE PRESENT

★★★ **Fond Latisab Creole Park** (Sun to Fri tours by appointment; tel: 450 6327) is just a few miles south east of Babonneau via narrow country lanes in the small farming community of Fond Assau. The 4-ha (11-acre) working farm, which grows nutmeg, cocoa and cinnamon and produces its own honey from bees kept in hives on the land, lies between the Marquis and Louvet estates.

Fond Latisab maintains many aspects of traditional St Lucian culture, some of which stem back to the time when Amerindians inhabited the land, and practises farm techniques that have been passed on from father to son for hundreds of years. For example, local guides who live away from the property are alerted by drumbeat when they are needed. Even though there is a phone on the farm, much communication is done using the ancient art of drumming.

Visitors can watch log sawing done to the beating of drums accompanied by a *chak chak* band (named after the sound made by a local instrument). Log sawing by traditional method requires two men with skill rather than brute force to work the 3-kg (6-lb) tool. While sawing, the men sing Creole folk songs, accompanied by the band and the drum beats, which help to keep a rhythm and maintain momentum. You can also see local people crayfishing, using traditional bamboo pots *(see page 46)*; and making cassava bread and farine – a fine cassava flour obtained from the root vegetable grown on the estate. The cast-iron pots used to mix flour for the bread were made at the Vauxhall Foundry in Liverpool, England, around the late 17th and early 18th centuries. Cassava bread is on sale here when there is a tour, and home-grown nutmeg and cinnamon can also be purchased.

## A FAR EASTERN DETOUR

Northwest of Babonneau, the winding Allan Bousquet Highway follows the Choc River, passing through land occupied by a power station and water works about 2.5 km (1½ miles) away.

Eventually, it leads to the ★ **Union Nature Trail** (daily 9am–4pm; no guided tours at the weekend; entrance fee), on an outpost of the Forestry and Lands Department. The walking trail loop begins on a path near the ranger station and can be covered in about an hour. It is a short walk (1.6 km/1 mile) through dry forest with a few small hills, and can be enjoyed by any relatively fit visitor, young or old.

The collection of wildlife on the property is not extensive, but it includes native species such as agouti and the St Lucia parrot, which few visitors see in the wild. There is also a small but interesting herb garden, which has many plants with medicinal properties that are used in herbal medicine as traditional cures.

**Star Attraction**
● **Fond Latisab Creole Park**

**Creole culture**
Fond Latisab Creole Park is part of a network of sites across the island that are members of the St Lucia Heritage Tourism Programme, which aims to encourage local communities to preserve and develop environmentally sensitive and sustainable tourist attractions.

## FROM GREAT HOUSE TO GRANDE ANSE

Back in Babonneau head northeast, this time to enjoy a landscape of sweeping valleys divided by rivers. The **Marquis Estate** (tours by appointment only; tel: 450 5436) sits in one such valley with stands of teak, coffee and cocoa. The fertile soil and a ready water supply on its border from the Marquis River made the plantation an 18th-century success story for its French owners. The estate is still a working farm, and although the great house is not open to the public, there are

*Nutmeg and mace*

Map
on pages
34–5

*The leatherback (Demochelys coriacea) is the world's largest turtle*

organised walking tours of the property, which extends east to the coast where the river flows into the ocean.

South of the river is the beautiful beach at ★★★**Grande Anse**, best known as a seasonal nesting site for the endangered leatherback turtle *(Demochelys coriacea)*. The valley in which this bay sits is thought to have historical significance because of the archaeological artefacts that have been discovered here, such as Amerindian petroglyphs, pottery shards and tools. The beach at Grande Anse, which along with the area's mangroves is part of a marine reserve, is best approached from Castries and the west on the highway to Babonneau and then southeast on a minor road to the village of Des Barra. The quiet beach is just east of the village.

## TURTLE WATCHING

Those willing to brave the poor roads will find a bay with a rocky landscape and a secluded 2-km (1¼-mile) strip of sand, which has reportedly been the target of illegal sand-miners. During the nesting season there have also been attempts to take valuable nesting turtles and their eggs. The sea around the bay is rough and strong winds can whip up the water, so it isn't safe to swim here, but a walk along the shore is a reward in itself.

From March to August the beach is monitored by the **Des Barras Grande Anse Turtle Watch Programme** *(see Introduction, page 9)*, a community group that works in conjunction with the St Lucia Naturalists' Society and the Ministry of Agriculture, Forestry and Fisheries. There are organised guided patrols of the beach to monitor the turtles, their nests and eggs during the nesting season. The group is also involved in education and conservation projects on the island.

According to a report by the Ministry, several other species of marine turtle, including the hawksbill turtle *(Eretmochelys imbricata)* and the green turtle *(Chelonia mydas)*, travel long distances to the protected bay here and elsewhere in St Lucia.

**Star Attraction**
● Grande Anse

### Turtle watch
The turtle watch patrols on Grande Anse beach begin in the early evening and continue until the following morning. The tours, which are part of the St Lucia Heritage Tourism Programme (tel: 451 6058 or 452 5067), are led by guides from the local community and welcome visitors from home and abroad. The tour includes an overnight camping session; participants are expected to supply their own food and drink.

## TURTLE HANGOUT
Sea turtles will only leave the water to dig deep in the sand to lay their eggs; once that task is complete they return to the ocean. This is a crucial time, when the nests and eggs must remain undisturbed for around 60 days to allow the young to hatch.

In an attempt to protect the endangered turtle population it is prohibited to touch or remove the eggs, the hatchlings or a nesting turtle.

## CACTI AND FOREST
The beach lies at the edge of the Grande Anse Estate, formerly a vast plantation spanning 810 ha (2,000 acres). Today, much of the estate lands are wild and uncultivated with cacti and dry forest peppering the hills and cliffs, providing a habitat for colourful birds that include the St Lucia wren *(Troglodytes aedon mesoluecos)*, the St Lucia oriole *(Icterus laudabilis)* and the white-breasted thrasher *(Ramphocinclus bracyurus sanctae luciae)*. Snakes, such as the poisonous fer-de-lance *(Bothrops caribbeae)* and boa constrictor *(constrictor orophias)*, and the protected iguana *(Iguana iguana)* also form part of the estate's endemic wildlife group.

*Sea turtles nest and lay their eggs on St Lucia's east coast beaches*

Map
on pages
58–9

👁 **Hardwood forest**
Southwest of Anse La Raye is a large forest area that forms part of the Anse Galet Estate. This hardwood forest includes stands of tall evergreens.

# 3: Marigot Bay and Roseau Valley

**Castries – Cul de Sac Valley – La Croix – Marigot Bay – Roseau Valley – Millet – Anse La Raye**

Leaving downtown Castries behind, travellers heading south will discover the verdant St Lucian countryside opens up with wide expanses of farmland bordered by dense forest and laced by rivers. The Millennium Highway leads south out of Castries and towards the West Coast Road, it's a well-made road, relatively smooth but winding in places. As the road climbs up into the hills that signal the outskirts of the capital, you can look back at the view of Morne Fortune and Castries below.

Within minutes, the beginning of the semi-industrial area of the **Cul de Sac Valley** appears. At the side of the highway is a green space known as the Millennium Park, used as an open-air venue for a variety of festivities including New Year celebrations. In the bay beyond the park is a natural deep harbour and what was once a vast terminal for Hess Oil. For the moment the storage facility remains unused. Trees and farms border the road to the left, carpeting the land with fields of banana trees and other crops, while the Cul de Sac River cuts a path from the dense forested interior, meandering west to **Grande Cul de Sac Bay** where it flows into the Caribbean Sea.

*Inspecting a banana plantation in the Cul de Sac Valley*

## GOING BANANAS

At the end of the Millennium Highway the West Coast Road starts to climb past the Lucelec power station, which provides the main electricity supply to the greater part of the island, and a little further still is the small village of La Croix on the edge of the rainforest. From the village plantation land stretches away into the distance, this is the ★★**Roseau Valley**. The sprawling Roseau Plantation is reported to have extended over what are now the Roseau and the Cul de Sac valleys.

At the heart of the plantation area is the small village of **Roseau** which stands near farmland once owned by Geest before it was broken up and taken over by individual farmers. Today many of the farms form part of an agricultural collective providing bananas for European supermarkets *(see page 15)*. This is one of St Lucia's main banana producing regions and here is the largest banana plantation on the island. Fields and fields of the fruit trees cover the land almost as far as the eye can see.

**Star Attraction**
● Roseau Valley

## SUGAR AND RUM

Before bananas, sugar was the agricultural mainstay and it is this crop that transformed the lush river valleys in the 18th century. The demand for sugar and its by-products from Europe and further afield resulted in St Lucian farmers planting acres of the labour-intensive sugar cane. So, along with the other neighbouring Caribbean islands, landowners here imported vast numbers of enslaved men and women, originating from West Africa, to carry out the back-breaking work on the land.

Successful for a time, St Lucia was forced to diversify in the mid-20th century following the introduction to Europe of cheaper sugar produced from sugar beet and due to fierce competition from high-volume sugar producers elsewhere in the Caribbean. The Roseau sugar refinery struggled on but eventually it too gave up; it was one of the last sugar factories to close in 1963.

*Western St Lucia is farming and fishing country*

Map
on pages
58–9

## A PICTURESQUE HARBOUR

Before continuing south towards another of Roseau's attractions, why not take a detour. Travel in a northerly direction for less than 1 km (⅔ mile) for spectacular views over the surrounding hills and picturesque harbour. The road climbs north-west through the valley and at the next left turn the route follows up a steep hill before it descends to ★★★ **Marigot Bay**. During the day the bay feels a little isolated and away from it all, though only 5 km (3 miles) from Castries centre, and that's part of its enduring attraction.

There is a small palm-fringed beach and a sheltered natural harbour, which includes The Moorings, a yacht and sailing base and equipment facility, making the bay a popular choice among local sailors and visitors who spend the winter in the Caribbean. On the south side of the bay the hills are peppered with luxury hotels and palatial homes and villas, some available for rent *(see page 117)*.

*Below: rum, the spirit of St Lucia*
*Bottom: on the beach at Marigot Bay*

## NORTH SIDE OF THE BAY

The north side of the bay is accessible only by boat, but that small detail doesn't appear to put people off: Marigot Bay is well known for its lively nightlife and the north side is dotted with a healthy number of bars and restaurants. As the evening

descends the traffic across the bay increases with boats sailing to-and-fro, and an inexpensive and regular ferry (water taxi) service operates 24 hours per day. The water around the bay where the Marigot Beach Club Hotel and Dive Resort (tel: 451 4974) is located is ideal for swimming and the resort also fronts the area's best beach. Visitors are drawn to the place primarily because of its pretty location but also for its restaurant, Doolittle's, named after the film that was shot here in the 1960s.

But it's not all flashy resorts and alfresco dining around the bay. The eastern part of the lagoon has a mangrove swamp, a natural site that has been protected with reserve status. Nearby St Lucian-owned and operated JJ's Paradise Resort has a busy bar, serves local Creole dishes and offers accommodation in pretty wooden cottages.

## A Rum Business

Cane sugar production fuelled the rum industry on the island. The ★ ★ **Roseau Distillery** (call for tour times; tel: 451 4315/4528) still produces a wide selection of colourful and fiery rums and liqueurs. One of the better known is the powerful Denros, named after the areas that produce the sugar to make the drink – the plantations in the eastern quarter of Dennery and Roseau (Den-Ros). Other brands produced here include Bounty and Old Fort, which are staples in the shops and bars.

The distillery, which is just off the main road, is signposted and not hard to find from the West Coast Road. Travelling from north to south, pass the Marigot Bay turn and continue until you reach a junction, take a right along a short, rough road, which is not much wider than an unmade path (muddy in the rain). One side is lined with a handful of small wooden homes and a shop, and at the end is the rum factory. Here you will find a visitors' centre, a shop and an old warehouse. This was also the site of a 19th-century, steam-powered sugar mill, with a narrow-gauge railway and steam engine used to transport the cane and molasses. Today only a steam train and a hoist

**Star Attractions**
● Marigot Bay
● Roseau Distillery

**Talk to the animals**
Marigot Bay was immortalised on the silver screen when it was used as a location for the Hollywood film, *Dr Dolittle*, in 1967. Rex Harrison starred in the movie.

*Everything you need for a day at Marigot Bay*

Map on pages 58–9

Map on pages 58–9

👁 **West coast wind down**
The fish fry at Anse La Raye is popular with tourists and locals alike. People come to unwind at the end of the week and it is generally free of trouble.

*Fishing boats at Anse La Raye*

remain, but they give an idea of the kind of heavy machinery that was needed to haul the sugar cane and produce large quantities of rum for the domestic and export markets.

The distillery organises lively guided tours showing how rum was made in the past and how it is produced using modern techniques, ending with a sample nip or two of the local firewater.

The small hill community of **Jacmel**, which lies east of the Roseau Valley, has a church with a striking altar decoration by the contemporary St Lucian artist Dunstan St Omer. Best visited with a local guide, as even in daylight the winding, narrow roads are difficult to negotiate.

## A FISHING TRADITION

The West Coast Road carves a direct route south through the plateau of the Roseau Valley, its banana plantations and the surrounding rolling hills to Soufrière. The road links small rural villages and as you near the coast the farming communities that produce bananas and cassava give way to sleepy fishing hamlets.

The journey weaves through the historically important village of Massacré and descends down to sleepy ★★ **Anse La Raye**. At first glance there isn't much to recommend the village; its narrow streets are lined with nondescript small shops and residences. But at the entrance to the village there is a sign pointing the way towards the small **Anse La Raye waterfall**, reachable with the help of a local guide by a short walk through the undergrowth. Sadly, no swimming is allowed at these falls.

The village itself has a police station, a community centre, a Catholic church and a filling station, while along the sea front small brightly painted fishing boats bob at their moorings in the water and fishermen's huts on the beach provide shelter and shade for repairing a seine (net) or just shooting the breeze. The pace is relaxed and as people go about their daily business visitors can get a sense of the real St Lucia without the tourist gloss.

## FRIDAY FISH FRY

Friday evening is a different story altogether, for this is when the village wakes up and comes alive with a Friday fish fry. The event is almost a precursor to the Gros Islet Jump-up on the northwest coast *(see page 40)*, but Anse La Raye's is a much more relaxed affair with families coming along. In the early evening the road is blocked off as stallholders set up coal pots and barbecues in front of the fishermen's huts and lay out tables so that people can enjoy their meal in the open air while they soak up the atmosphere. By 9pm the place is packed and loud music punctuates the air while locals and visitors alike walk the length of the road to see what's on offer before making a choice from a variety of dishes. On sale are fish most likely caught that day by local fishermen, such as red snapper, kingfish and dolphin (dorado or mahi-mahi) along with potfish, conch salad, breadfruit salad and floats and bakes (similar to fried dumplings), washed down with a Piton beer or soft drink. The village bars are also busy with the usual end-of-the-week crowd swelled by people at the fish fry. Some very basic public facilities are available near the fishermen's huts.

It's not unusual to start the weekend chilling out at Anse La Raye fish fry and then later in the evening to go on to a local bar or head up north to the Jump-up at Gros Islet.

**Star Attraction**
● Anse La Raye

*Below: Marigot Bay*
*Bottom: the art of Dunstan St Omer in a Jacmel church*

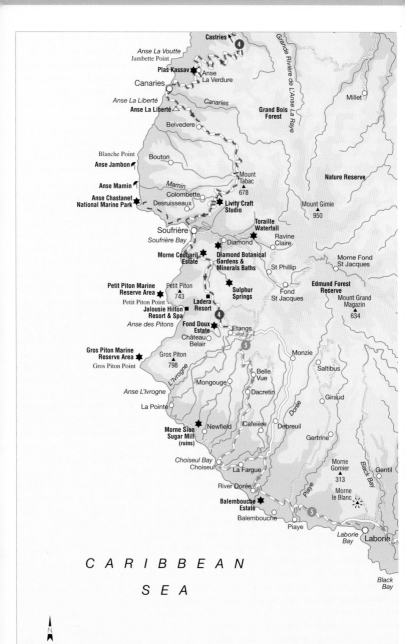

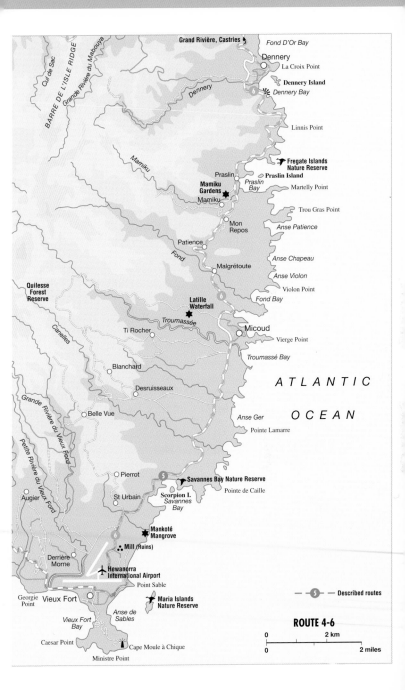

Cul de Sac

BARRE DE L'ISLE RIDGE

Grande Rivière du Mabouya

Grand Rivière, Castries

Fond D'Or Bay

Dennery

Dennery

La Croix Point

**Dennery Island**

Dennery Bay

Linnis Point

Mamiku

Praslin

**Fregate Islands
Nature Reserve**

**Praslin Island**

**Mamiku
Gardens**

Praslin
Bay

Martelly Point

Mamiku

Trou Gras Point

Mon
Repos

Anse Patience

Patience

Fond

Anse Chapeau

Malgrétoute

Anse Violon

Violon Point

**Quilesse
Forest
Reserve**

**Latille
Waterfall**

Fond Bay

Troumassée

Micoud

Ti Rocher

Vierge Point

Canelles

Blanchard

Troumassé Bay

Desruisseaux

A T L A N T I C

Belle Vue

O C E A N

Grande Rivière du Vieux Ford

Anse Ger

Pointe Lamarre

Petite Rivière du Vieux Ford

Pierrot

Savannes Bay Nature Reserve

Pointe de Caille

Augier

St Urbain

**Scorpion I.**
Savannes
Bay

**Mankoté
Mangrove**

**Mill (Ruins)**

Derrière
Morne

**Hewanorra
International Airport**

Point Sable

Georgie
Point

Vieux Fort

**Maria Islands
Nature Reserve**

Anse de
Sables

Vieux Fort
Bay

Caesar Point

Cape Moule à Chique

Ministre Point

— ─ 5 ─ — **Described routes**

**ROUTE 4-6**

0        2 km

0        2 miles

Map
on pages
58–9

# 4: Soufrière and the West Coast

**Castries – Canaries – Soufrière – Anse Chastanet – Diamond Botanical Gardens – La Soufrière Sulphur Springs – Petit Piton – Gros Piton**

**Cassava bread**

If you want to take some cassava bread home, the best way to preserve it is to freeze it. Buy the bread as close to your departure date as possible, but leave enough time for it to freeze solid. Once frozen, wrap it up well and transport it in a cool bag. Eat within a day of defrosting.

The journey south from Castries to Soufrière, along the West Coast, goes from urban to countryside in less than two hours. Though tiny, even by Caribbean standards, the island encompasses a wide variety of landscapes from open plains to rolling hills and valleys, ragged mountain ranges and lush rainforest. The West Coast Road is well made and the stretch from the capital through the Roseau Valley is fairly easy to negotiate. But as the road descends to Anse La Raye and beyond, it twists and turns requiring skilful and careful driving. In places you can see that the road has been literally cut through the hills and is shaded by mature trees and vegetation, while farms and fishing villages dot the panorama below.

## LA SIKWI'S SWEET HISTORY

On the outskirts of Anse La Raye a path leads to a restored sugar mill south of the village, just before the bridge that stretches across the Grande Rivière de L'Anse La Raye. ★ **La Sikwi Sugar Mill** (entrance fee; tel: 452-6323), which is sometimes used for weddings and other functions, was constructed in about 1860 on the original Invergoil Estate. The mill, which once ground sugar cane to extract the juice for sugar and its by-products, can be reached by a short 15-minute walk through undergrowth, and is best attempted with a guide.

*Cassava is a St Lucian staple.*

The current estate owners have tried to keep a naturalness about the land where shady trails circle the lush gardens full of bright blooms and a cooling 15-m (50-ft) waterfall that is a popular spot with local children, who also play by the river nearby. Although the mill is no longer operational, it is in good condition with a large wheel and other components and conveys a sense of the backbreaking and monotonous life of slaves and farm labourers. The plantation used to be one of the island's successful sugar producers. Later other crops, such as cocoa, took precedence maintaining the estate's profits. A bar and restaurant opens when there are enough visitors.

## A ST LUCIAN SPECIALITY

On the route south the road winds sharply as it cuts its way through the undulating hills down to the valley. In places there are stunning views of the coast and the Pitons – Gros Piton and Petit Piton – as the road skirts along the cliffs with a sheer drop to dense vegetation below. Elsewhere, as the road widens, the homes of local people are set back slightly, then in a curve in the road, opposite a stand of trees at Anse La Verdue, is ★ **Plas Kassav** (daily 8.30am–7 or 8pm).

*Below: hill country*
*Bottom: fishermen repair their boats on the west coast*

This family bakery uses traditional methods and some innovative equipment to produce farine (from cassava) and a mouth-watering variety of cassava bread that is popular with local workers, especially at lunchtime. Several cruise ships and organised tours make this a regular stop, providing people with an opportunity to taste one of the island's specialities, and you can buy some to take back home.

Attached to the bakery is a small shop that sells refreshments and cassava bread in a choice of flavours including peanut, cherry, raisin, sweet,

Map on pages 58–9

salt, saltfish and smoked herring. The bread makes a hearty snack or can be used as an accompaniment to a meal.

## FISHING, FOREST AND FURNITURE

A few minutes drive from Anse La Verdue the road winds its way down to **Canaries** (pronounced can-ar-ees), a small village where most families eke out a living from the fruits of the sea. There is some discussion about where the village's name originates – is it from seafarers who originally hailed from the Canary Islands or named after an Amerindian utensil used by the Arawak-speaking peoples who settled here; archaeological discoveries in the surrounding district support the latter theory.

The **Canaries River** flows through the forest and out to sea here, supporting a handful of waterfalls to the south of the village. Most are hard to find without a guide and require a 30-minute hike, at the very least, to reach them.

Only a few minutes south of Canaries off the West Coast Road is the **Anse La Liberté campsite** (tel: 453-7656/5014), the only one on the island. A large roadside sign heralds the entrance to the camp so it's not difficult to find. The campsite extends 54 ha (133 acres) into forest land managed by the St Lucia National Trust. It

*Below: camp St Lucian-style at Anse La Liberté*
*Bottom: the Pitons*

has around 6 km (4 miles) of walking trails, a strip of good beach and basic facilities. The site can also be accessed by water taxi from Canaries.

⭐

**Star Attraction**
● Livity Craft Studio

## SHADED RETREAT

Inland and east of Canaries, near Belvedere, is **Grand Bois Forest**. Views of the cool and shady vegetation can be seen from the winding road and the forest is the habitat of several endemic plant species and wildlife, with mature stands of bamboo, palms and tropical fern.

As the road snakes through the hills you can enjoy stunning views of the sea and the spectacular western landscape backed by the magnificent Pitons, which dominate the area, lying just beyond the centre of Soufrière. But before that **Mount Tabac** comes into view, rising high above the hills and forests to its 678-m (2,224-ft) peak.

In **Colombette**, before the road begins its descent to the next town, don't miss ★★**Livity Craft Studio**. The work of two local artists, who are part of an artists' cooperative, is on sale here. The artisans relocated from Choiseul in the south. Look out for hand-crafted furniture such as beautiful white cedar chairs, calabash bowls and basketwork from the Edge & Livity line, adorned with hand-painted designs.

> 👁 **Bay of Freedom**
> Anse La Liberté, the bay after which the island's only campsite is named, is thought to have historical significance. It is believed that enslaved men and women celebrated their emancipation here in 1834, hence the name – Anse La Liberté (Bay of Freedom).

## SOUFRIERE

The rural west is an antidote to the hustle and bustle of the capital; life moves at a much slower pace here. The journey from Castries to Soufrière takes about an hour and a quarter, even though the distance between the two places is only about 32 km (20 miles). The road along the West Coast, heading north to south, is winding and potholed in places once you leave the Millennium Highway just outside Castries. You must have your wits about you if you intend to drive yourself because these mountain roads can be unforgiving, with steep drops down to the valley below.

Map
on page
63

Map on page 63

**Driving**
Drive at your own pace, allow local drivers to pass you as you take your time and reach your destination safely. It's best to opt for an automatic hire car, which will help when driving along the narrow twisting mountain roads. If you want to drive in the deep rural areas where the roads are steep and more than often poorly maintained, be sure to rent a sturdy four-wheel drive.

## ST LUCIA'S OLDEST TOWN

The road twists, rises and falls towards the sea and the heart of the West Coast, surrounded by mountains and dense protected forests and lapped by clear waters that shelter spectacular dive sites. Just before you reach the town of Soufrière a sign marks the turn off for **Le Haut Plantation**, about 2 km (1¼ miles) away. The restaurant on the 20-ha (52-acre) estate is a popular place, and not just for the breathtaking views; there is also a bar and a few rooms for rent. Several viewpoints are marked along the West Coast Road where you can stop to look down over the picturesque bay, especially pretty if there is a tall ship in the harbour.

Established in the 18th century, ★★ **Soufrière** is St Lucia's oldest town and was the capital when France controlled the island. It stands in the shadow of the island's most striking and best-known landmark – the Pitons. Louis XIV of France granted around 809 ha (2,000 acres) of land to the Du Boulay family, who ran a successful plantation growing sugar, cocoa, tobacco and cotton on the estate. Descendants of the family still own land and property in the area today.

## SOUFRIERE'S LAYOUT

For many years after the country was ceded to the British, Soufrière remained little more than a small fishing village, but today it is expanding. The population of the village proper and its environs is now believed to be close to 8,000.

Enter the village via a small bridge over the **Soufrière River**, which flows to the sea just to the west. On the left is a Shell petrol station (cash only), to the right is the town hall and after that, business and residential properties line both sides of Bridge Street, the main road. Heading south turn right into Sir Darnley Alexander Street and then left into Maurice Mason Street to reach the waterfront. Facing the small harbour is the police station, the post office, and a gift shop, which sells souvenirs and a selection of items made by local artists. Also on this road is the tourist information office and another petrol station (Texaco).

*Seine, sea and Piton*

## COLONIAL ARCHITECTURE

Modern and colonial buildings stand side by side; painted in pastels, many have pretty balconies with gingerbread fretwork. Most notable is the **Old Courthouse** at the southern end of the water-front. Constructed in 1898, the historic stone, colonial-style building has a veranda restaurant called the Scales of Justice, a bar and, upstairs, the art gallery (tel: 459 5002) displays sculptures, batiks and paintings by local artists.

Near to the jetty is the **St Lucia Tourist Information Office** (Mon to Fri 8am–4pm, Sat 8am–noon) where the staff are helpful and friendly. The office is a good place to go for advice on tours of the area and recommendations for local guides.

The waterfront has a small paved area with seats looking out across the harbour, which is often dominated by the large sail-assisted ships that frequent the port for a few hours. The deep harbour drops to 60 m (200 ft) close to shore so Windjammer yachts and sailing ships can dock right at the pier, while the larger Star Clippers drop anchor just outside and tender passengers to dry land. A common sight here is the Brig *Unicorn*, which regularly brings passengers on day trips from Castries. The tall ship was used in *Roots*, a TV series based on the Pulitzer prize-winning book of the same name written by the late Alex Haley.

**Star Attraction**
● **Soufrière**

*A pretty Soufrière balcony and boats in the busy harbour*

Map on page 63

*Children in the town square with the Lady of Assumption in the background*

## SOUFRIERE MARINE MANAGEMENT AREA

At the northern end of the pier is another jetty, the **Soufrière Marine Management Area** (SMMA) office and a water taxi station and tour office where you can book transport around the coast. Visitors can go to places that are difficult to reach by road, and also to some of the island's best dive sites, as well as join boat trips around the Pitons.

The SMMA, which extends from Anse Jambon to Anse L'Ivrogne almost at the foot of Gros Piton, was established in 1994 to protect the unique marine habitat along the West Coast of St Lucia. It regularly monitors the coral reefs and water quality, carrying out scientific research in an attempt to prevent damage to reefs, fish stock, beaches and vegetation as Soufrière and its environs along the West Coast continue to develop.

Its four main protected Marine Reserve Areas (MRAs), for which you will require a permit to dive, are:
● Anse Chastanet
● Rachette Pointe
● Petit Piton
● Gros Piton (restricted access)

Permits can be purchased on an annual or daily basis and are available from the SMMA (tel: 459 5500) and authorised dive operators.

## EXPLORING SOUFRIERE

Soufrière can be easily explored on foot; there are few sights, and most are within a few minutes' walk of the water. Most of the area's attractions are either on, or underneath the water, or in and around the rainforest. What the town does have is atmosphere. A handful of vendors sell local produce from the street around the corner from the tourist office, and on Saturday there is a busy street market for early risers near the waterfront.

The airy **Lady of Assumption Church**, built in the 1950s, stands at the corners of Henry Belmar, Sir Arthur Lewis and Boulevard streets. It has a simple design with the lovely altar and pulpit made from dark tropical wood. Above the main doors is a magnificent pipe organ.

## TOWN SQUARE HUSTLERS

Just in front of the church steps is the **town square** where a guillotine was erected by Brigands *(see pages 32–3)* during the French Revolution. If you wander through the small square be aware that this is one place where there is relatively high unemployment. You may be solicited for money or be approached by an unofficial (and unwanted) guide offering to show you around the church; a guide is not necessary, so a firm but polite refusal should suffice. If you do want a guide to show you around town, ask the staff at the tourist office or your hotel to recommend a reliable one. On the north side of the square, on Henry Belmar Street, you will find buses for Castries and on the south side, on Sir Arthur Lewis Street, are buses for Vieux Fort and the south.

**Star Attraction**
● Anse Chastanet

**An impressive tall ship**
The Brig *Unicorn* was built in 1946 and is a replica of a ship from 1850. The brig has masts 30-m (100-ft) tall carrying 600 sq m (6,500 sq ft) of sail needing 5 km (3 miles) of rope *(see page 65)*. Tours run from Castries to Soufrière.

## DIVING DELIGHT

★★★ **Anse Chastanet** is a national marine park and well-known dive area just north of Soufrière, but the access road is potholed and narrow so you would be best advised to take a water taxi around the bay. To reach the beach from Soufrière by road, travel back as if returning to Castries, but just as you cross the bridge on the edge of town veer left. It's a tortuous 15-minute journey but it's well worth it.

*Soufrière has colourful marine life, ideal for diving*

Map on pages 58–9

**👁 Protect the reefs**

•Do not damage or touch the coral while you are snorkelling or diving.

• Do not remove any plants, animals, fish or even shells from the sea.

• Do not feed the fish.

• Tie up only to mooring buoys or anchor at official sandy areas.

• Do not buy souvenirs made from coral; it is illegal to remove it from St Lucia.

• Do not buy souvenirs or other items made from turtle shells.

• Do not litter; dispose of waste in the appropriate bins.

*Choose an active holiday.*

The Anse Chastanet Resort dominates the beaches and 243 ha (600 acres) of verdant land here. Spacious and luxurious tree-house style, open-air rooms built in to the hillside look out to the Pitons, and a dive operation, **Scuba St Lucia**, rents snorkelling and scuba-diving equipment. PADI and NAUI scuba courses are available for everyone, from beginners to the more experienced.

Volcanic black sand fronts the hotel, while the ★★ **Anse Chastanet reef**, with a host of colourful marine life, offers the opportunity to literally walk to a dive site within a few metres of the shore. Divers and snorkellers are treated to bright displays of coral, sponges, angelfish, parrot fish and seahorses.

## BEACHES AND WATERFALLS

North of Anse Chastanet are two fine golden sand beaches, ★★ **Anse Mamin** and ★★ **Anse Jambon**. Anse Mamin is ideal for a picnic or a day spent relaxing on the beach and dipping your toes in the clear water. The beach is backed by forest and former plantation land from where **Bike St Lucia** organises energetic cycling trips, known as jungle biking, along 19 km (12 miles) of bike trails through the 17th-century plantation.

East of Soufrière, on the way to the forested interior, is ★★ **Toraille Waterfall** (entrance fee). The falls cascade 15 m (50 ft) over a cliff and into a cool pool surrounded by colourful flora and shady trees. The strength of the water flow depends on how much rain has fallen, but even after a dry spell it is still worth a look. A wooden walkway leads from the entrance to the pool.

Although the waterfall nestles in a sharp bend in the road in a deep ravine, it is difficult to catch a glimpse of it from outside the property because Toraille is shielded by vegetation. The site is part of the island's Heritage Tourism programme, which aims to encourage the preservation of important sites and to encourage visits to small, interesting attractions. It is worth the small entrance fee.

On the other side of the road a fence protects sightseers from straying too far for a look over the steep cliff to the land below. On the east side of the ravine is **Mount Gimie**, which at more than 950 m (3,145 ft) high stands above both of the better-known peaks of the Pitons *(see page 75)*.

**Star Attraction**
● Diamond Botanical Gardens

## MINERAL BATHS AND FLOWERS

South of Soufrière, old estate houses and hotels populate the hillsides, mostly shielded from the road by magnificent trees and bordered by fertile farmland. Head east out of town on Sir Arthur Lewis Street and a few kilometres along a good road you will reach the ★★★ **Diamond Botanical Gardens, Mineral Baths and Waterfall** (Mon to Sat 10am–5pm, Sun and public hols. 10am–3pm; entrance fee; tel: 459 7565). Originally part of the Soufrière Estate, the gardens were developed and the baths built in 1784 by the Governor of St Lucia, Baron de Laborie, after it was discovered that water from the sulphur springs was mineral rich and an effective treatment for rheumatism and other ailments. The baths were constructed on the instruction of the French King Louis XVI for his troops, but they were destroyed during the French Revolution. The bathing pools were restored in 1925 and facilities were expanded in 2002 providing visitors

*Below: colourful orchids*
*Bottom: the beach at Anse Chastanet*

Map on pages 58–9

with the choice of bathing in a communal outdoor pool or individual baths for an additional fee. The waterfall lies beyond the mineral baths and a small shop sells reasonably priced souvenirs and snacks.

## A GARDEN TRAIL

A short trail snakes through the botanical gardens and useful and descriptive signs identify tropical flora such as fragrant frangipani, red ginger, vibrant hibiscus and a variety of trees laden with coconut, cocoa or other local staples, so a guide is not necessary. A longer and more strenuous hike, which crosses over the **Diamond River**, leads to the old mill and a working waterwheel.

## PLANTATION LIFE

★★**Morne Coubaril Estate** (daily 9am–4pm; entrance fee; guided tours; tel: 459 7340) lies less than 1 km (⅔ mile) from Soufrière on the Soufrière–Vieux Fort Road, almost opposite the slip road that leads to the vast and luxurious Jalousie Hilton.

The 113-ha (280-acre) working plantation is one of the oldest on the island. It was owned by the Deveaux family until 1960 when it was taken over by Donald Monplaisir. The Monplaisir family have attempted to restore and preserve the property and it's agricultural traditions. Although

*Surrounded by bright flora at Diamond Botanical Gardens*

the great house is not open to the public because it remains a family home, visitors can view the exterior of the building, which has been extended by the present owners and is in excellent condition with lovely wrap-around verandas.

Colourful flora and trees heavy with fruit such as papaya, banana, coconut, orange and grapefruit grow in abundance. There are also cocoa trees and if you are lucky you may get the chance to taste the sweet pulp that surrounds the seeds inside the cocoa pod.

## WALKS AND TALKS

Fascinating walking tours of the property take in the Copra House, where coconuts are prepared for sale to the St Lucia Coconut Growers Association, which produces coconut oil, and there is a lovely view over the deep bay nearby. You can also see a fully operational sugar mill where a mule is used to turn the wheel that grinds the sugar cane and produces the juice to make sugar and rum.

Plantation work was back-breaking and the enslaved Africans and farm labourers endured a hard life. Replica wooden slave quarters reveal how people were forced to live in basic and cramped conditions. The huts have been reconstructed using traditional methods, with mud and paper on the walls and palm thatch on the roof.

Morne Coubaril also organises trekking expeditions on horseback (by appointment) and a choice of rainforest hikes (up to 3 hours) that visit the **Coubaril waterfall**, which is fed by the Sulphur Springs. Though strenuous, the walks are fun with an informative guide and reach a lookout point that provides a panoramic view over Soufrière.

## 'DRIVE-IN' VOLCANO

Beyond Morne Coubaril plantation, off the Soufrière–Vieux Fort Road are ★★ **La Soufrière Sulphur Springs** (daily 9am–5pm; entrance fee), promoted as the world's only drive-in volcano, which isn't strictly true – visitors can drive up

**Star Attractions**
- Morne Coubaril
- Sulphur Springs

**Scientific research**
The Sulphur Springs are believed to be the hottest geothermal area in the Lesser Antilles. Scientists carry out a variety of research at the springs, such as its potential as a geothermal energy source. They have recorded temperatures of more than 170°C (338°F) from fumaroles (steam vents).

*A colourful country cottage on Morne Coubaril Estate*

Map on pages 58–9

**Battle of Rabot**

The Fond Doux Estate is close to the site of the Battle of Rabot, fought in 1795, when freedom fighters forced the British military to retreat outside Soufrière. The previous year, the new French Republic had granted freedom to enslaved Africans in its foreign territories. But when St Lucia was again brought under British influence the emancipated islanders feared they would be returned to bondage, hence the resulting rebellion.

*Drying cocoa beans at the Fond Doux Estate*

to the car park and then walk in. As you approach the site you can smell the pungent odour (hydrogen sulphide), not dissimilar to rotten eggs. At times, when a strong wind blows and the vapours are high, the whiff can be detected at quite a distance.

La Soufrière volcano is no longer active; it collapsed more than 40,000 years ago and now produces only the foul-smelling gases and hot water that can reach temperatures of 135°C (275°F). At the ticket booth, be prepared for vendors who congregate here to offer their wares; guides also wait to escort visitors, for an additional fee, down a wooden pathway and along some uneven ground.

To the right, the rocky landscape of the geothermal field looks like something from a science-fiction movie, with springs and grey-brown mud bubbling up sporadically. Be careful when you are on the walkway as the mud and water that gurgles and gloops is hot. A good guide will give you a rundown of the site and its history and should be able to answer any questions you have.

## FRUITFUL FOND DOUX

Back on the main road, south of the springs, is the ★★ **Fond Doux Estate** (open daily; entrance fee; tel: 459 7545), another working plantation that is worth a visit. An inexpensive guided tour includes a look inside the original plantation house, built in 1864 and renovated in the 1990s, which is currently occupied. Adjacent to the estate house is a colonial-style restaurant, a bar and a souvenir shop. The grounds, which extend over 55 ha (135 acres), are planted with coffee, banana, mango, citrus fruits and coconut and there is also an original worker's house, store house, copra house and coffee-drying area.

Cocoa grown here is shipped to the United States for use in chocolate produced by the Hershey Food Corporation. A leisurely walk through the estate reveals an abundance of bright and fragrant flora such as heliconia and vibrant carpets of anthuriums.

## LUXURIOUS LODGINGS

Luxury hotels dot the southwest coast and valley from Soufrière, taking advantage of the spectacular views of the shoreline bound by rich vegetation, and nestling below the majestic peaks of Petit Piton and Gros Piton.

Back on the route along the Soufrière–Vieux Fort Road, opposite the entrance to Morne Coubaril a sign indicates an access road leading to the large all-inclusive **Jalousie Hilton Resort and Spa**. The approach road is not only narrow, but rises and dips at precarious angles, passing an artist's studio, residential houses and a small **waterfall** (entrance fee) where locals wait to offer unofficial guided services. Here too is an entrance to the **Stonefield Estate**, which has colourful rustic villas to rent and the Mango Tree Restaurant and Bar offering tasty local dishes and cocktails to be savoured in front of a wonderful view of the Pitons and the sea.

The road steepens as it approaches the resort, which opened amid a wave of controversy when local people, environmentalists and archaeologists objected to its location because of its proximity to the Pitons. Objections were also raised because it is built on an important Amerindian site; archaeologists have discovered crucial remnants here, and there is a petroglyph on the property.

**Star Attraction**
● Fond Doux Estate

*La Soufrière Sulphur Springs and volcano*

Map
on pages
58–9

The resort, which is partly government-owned, stands in a prime location that was once a copra estate in a pretty bay at the foot of the Pitons, where the stunning views account for its popularity with both honeymooners and families. Set in hilly grounds and with beautiful gardens, it has a lovely white beach created with imported sand and is a large employer of local people. On the complex are a variety of restaurants, including Bang Between the Pitons and a helipad for guests who travel light and prefer to avoid the sometimes difficult road journey from Hewanorra Airport.

## PICTURE PERFECT

A little way up the road is **Ladera Resort**, another luxury place to stay with excellent views. The beautiful accommodation, made predominantly of stone and dark tropical woods, is built into the hillside and open to the elements on one side. So guests not only have picture-perfect views of the Pitons and the green valley below, but can also benefit from the cooling breezes.

Ladera is home to the award-winning restaurant ★★**Dasheene**, named after the common root vegetable dasheen (also known as taro). Though expensive, the restaurant cuisine – Creole with a contemporary twist – is highly recommended and not to be missed.

*Ladera Resort overlooks the Pitons*

## SCALING THE PITONS

★★★ **The Pitons** dominate the southwestern landscape around Soufrière. **Petit Piton** (743 m/2,438 ft) is to the north of Soufrière harbour, while **Gros Piton** (798 m/2,618 ft) is on the south side of the bay near the L'Ivrogne River. The tall volcanic cones, which are covered in rich vegetation, are undoubtedly the most photographed rocks in St Lucia. Their image can be seen on everything from postcards to T-shirts and art.

For many people the Pitons offer pleasure simply for their sheer beauty. However, more adventurous spirits aren't satisfied with just looking at them – they want to get to the top. Though Petit Piton is the smaller of the two, it is more difficult to climb because of its steep sides, making climbing ropes essential. A relatively easier option is to hike up Gros Piton, although this isn't a walk in the park either. It is not a pursuit to be tackled alone and you will need to employ the services of a local guide. Contact the St Lucia Tourist office in Soufrière *(see page 65)* for guide recommendations, the Soufrière Regional Development Foundation (tel: 459 5500), or Gros Piton Guides Association (tel: 459 3492). Be prepared for a very early start – most guides recommend setting off and reaching your goal early in the morning before it gets too hot.

Scaling the peak can be hot and thirsty work in the tropical sun, so remember to bring plenty of water, sunblock and a suitable hat for shade. The time taken to complete the climb can vary; it is generally between three to six hours each way depending on the hiker's level of fitness.

## REWARDING VIEWS

The hike begins along an uneven path at the wide base of the rock and you may be able to spot a rare island bird, such as the St Lucian oriole, and other wildlife . Remember that you don't have to climb to the summit, but if you do you will be rewarded with sweeping panoramic views over the island, north and south and on a clear day as far as island neighbours Martinique and St Vincent.

**Star Attractions**
● **The Pitons**
● **Dasheene**

*Dishing out at Dasheene*

*Relax by the pool*

Map
on pages
58–9

**Second city**
Vieux Fort is considered to be St Lucia's second city, with a developing industrial centre and a population of 15,000.

# 5: Vieux Fort and the South

**Soufrière – Choiseul – Balenbouche – Vieux Fort – Cap Moule à Chique – Maria Islands Nature Reserve – Savannes Bay Nature Reserve**

The road south from Soufrière to Vieux Fort is akin to a winding obstacle course. It twists and turns in sharp bends and dips and rises through the hills and valleys, skirting forest and farmland, eventually passing through the small fishing hamlets that dot the southwestern coast.

## KEEP ON MOVING

Leaving Soufrière and its environs you will pass by a good many attractions covered in Route 4 *(see page 60)*. However, it can be quite an arduous journey to Vieux Fort, even though it isn't that far away, so for this itinerary, there is no time to dally; simply make a note of places that you might want to come back to and keep on going. To be sure you're travelling on the Etangs road in the direction of Saltibus, you should pass the slip road that leads to the Jalousie Hilton, the Fond Doux Estate and the Ladera Resort.

The trip southwest provides visitors with the chance to see rural St Lucia up close, enjoying views of the Pitons, particularly **Gros Piton** which sits on the edge of the district known as the Quarter of Choiseul. On a clear day, you may also catch a glimpse of neighbouring St Vincent's volcanic mountain, called La Soufrière too.

## UNTOUCHED LANDSCAPES

From Etangs the road turns through several small rural communities barely touched by tourism, and fertile land stretches out before you. On the coast road before you reach Newfield is a wide expanse of farmland that overlooks the sea, and nearby is a local landmark – the ruins of **Morne Sion Sugar Mill**, the only one of its kind on the island.

The West Coast Road to, and beyond, Choiseul is difficult to negotiate, but a major roadworks improvement programme is underway. While the

*A country car wash in the Balenbouche River*

work continues, diversions can extend your journey and take you off the beaten track, but things should improve quickly once it is complete.

## A TOWN OF ARTISANS

**Choiseul** is a good-size town with a developed centre that has a town hall, a church, several schools, a post office, petrol station and a community centre. The ruins of **Fort Citreon**, a fortress which protected Choiseul Bay, still stands guard over the area, but it is best known for ★★ **La Fargue Craft Centre**, where St Lucian artists have workshops and display their work. The centre is on the main drag and has parking spaces, so it's an ideal place to browse for authentic St Lucian-made products, such as clay pots, for which the area is well-known, basketwork, woodcarvings, local spices, seasonings and sauces.

The poor state of the roads in the past has forced several artists to relocate to areas more accessible to visitors, but there are still enough craftsmen based here to make a visit to the town worthwhile.

## BALENBOUCHE ESTATE

A few miles down the road is the ★★ **Balenbouche Estate** (daily; entrance fee; guided tours by appointment; tel: 455 1244), which stands

**Star Attractions**
● **La Fargue Craft Centre**
● **Balenbouche Estate**

*Balenbouche Estate house: exterior and interior views*

Map on pages 58–9

proudly between the Balenbouche and Piaye rivers. It is close by some important historical and archaeological sites, and nearby **Morne le Blanc** has a good lookout point.

## GREAT HOUSE

Balenbouche is about 30 minute's drive from Soufrière, in between Choiseul and Laborie. The first European settlement at Balenbouche was established in the mid-18th century when the land was cultivated and the original estate house was built.

*Below: Amerindian artefacts*
*Bottom: the ruins of the Balenbouche water wheel*

Today, the great house stands on the original site of two previous estate houses. Dating back from the mid-19th century and furnished with antiques from that period. The estate is a family-run guesthouse, restaurant and a working plantation. Visitors can walk along Balenbouche's nature trail or take a tour of the gardens that are one of the regular venues for concerts during the annual St Lucia Jazz Festival in May.

The land also includes a collection of ruins such as the slave quarters and the old plantation's sugar mill and water wheel with mechanical works that were shipped from England. The mill and the water wheel were used to process the sugar harvested on the plantation during the island's short-lived sugar boom.

There have been several significant archaeological discoveries on the estate, including pre-Columbian petroglyphs, ceramics and stone tools.

Two dark-coloured sandy beaches can be found at nearby **Balenbouche Bay**, just a five-minute walk from the estate, and **Anse Touloulu**, a little north of Balenbouche.

**Star Attraction**
● Vieux Fort

## FISHERMAN'S CHOICE

The journey continues south passing through **Laborie**, a small fishing community with wooden colonial-style buildings in its centre and a collection of modern fishing huts on the edge of the water. The village also has a pretty but quiet beach that is most often populated by a handful of local fishermen. Laborie has a small selection of accommodation for visitors who prefer to fish and stay close to nature and away from the crowds.

**In the beginning**
Hewanorra International Airport is named after an Amerindian word meaning "land of iguana". There have been significant archeological finds in the south of the island, where the airport is located.

## TO THE INDUSTRIAL ZONE

The West Coast road climbs out of Laborie up through the countryside and rural villages and then descends again into ★★ **Vieux Fort**, one of the oldest settlements at St Lucia's most southerly tip 67 km (42 miles) from Castries. This busy, modern industrial town is often the first sight of the island for visitors because **Hewanorra International Airport** is located here, on the plains that open out to the sea. There are a few hotels, mainly B&Bs, not too far from the airport, and some developed industry around the large port area, such as oil storage, warehouses and grain stores, and a wharf lined with shipping containers. Here, too, is one of the Eastern Caribbean's commercial-free-zone centres and a large fisheries complex, along with a bustling, if slightly haphazard, shopping area.

*English engineering*

## EXPLORING VIEUX FORT

It isn't difficult to get around Vieux Fort, especially near the airport, where the roads are wider and well signed; even in the older part of town

Map
on pages
58–9

*Above: French colonial architecture in Vieux Fort
Below: the deadly fer-de-lance snake*

which is full of small grocery stores, typical Caribbean shops, takeaways and bakeries. Modern villas rub shoulders with fading French colonial-style buildings, reflecting the historical origins of the town's first French settlers.

## WINDSURFERS' PARADISE

Vieux Fort has a beautiful strip of white-sand beach, **Anse de Sables**, part of which can be seen from the airport road. The waters just offshore are popular with windsurfers who come to take advantage of the trade winds that bless this coast. There is a little bar and restaurant and a surf centre, where boards and equipment can be rented. A little further north is a resort.

## LIGHTHOUSE WITH A VIEW

★★ **Cap Moule à Chique** is a rocky outcrop with dry forest that towers high above the town and is as far south as you can get on the mainland. A little way out of the town centre, a tall lighthouse stands above Vieux Fort, overlooking the southern coast of the island for miles. The drive up to the lighthouse requires a four-wheel drive and some nerve because of the twists and turns on the narrow path that leads up to a lookout, bordered by vegetation and sheer cliffs. Several residences dot the winding landscape and the peak up here, and at the top, next to the lighthouse is an electrical substation and a large antennae.

Standing at 223 m (730 ft) above sea level, the 9-m (29-ft) **lighthouse** tower is believed to be the second highest in the world, because of its location perched on top of Cap Moule à Chique. Painted white with a red lantern at the top, the tower itself is closed to the public but the lighthouse site is not. From here the view is spectacular: to the northwest, beyond Vieux Fort, are the rolling hills and valleys of the south, including the Pitons in the far distance, and **Morne Gomier**, a 313-m (1,028-ft) peak closer to town. While to the northeast, just off the coast, you will see the rocky Maria Islands Nature Reserve poking out of the sea like seals. Here, too, are sweeping views up around the East Coast, where the waves of the Caribbean Sea and Atlantic Ocean meet to buffet the land and the rocks below. On a clear day visitors to Cap Moule à Chique may also spot the north coast of St Vincent, which lies only 34 km (21 miles) away.

**Star Attractions**
● **Cap Moule à Chique**
● **Maria Islands Reserve**

## WILDLIFE ON THE ROCKS

★★**Maria Islands Nature Reserve** (closed during the summer breeding season mid-May to end of July) lies 1.5 km (1 mile) east of Vieux Fort, across a narrow ocean channel. From the mainland it looks as if the islands are nothing more than small rocky outcrops. However, the two largest islets, Maria Major and Maria Minor, form the main part of the nature reserve, which covers 12 ha (30 acres) of dry scrubland, characterised by a mixture of vegetation and cacti.

These compact islands on St Lucia's windward side have been shaped by the rough waves of the Atlantic, and are home to geckos and a stunning array of rare bird and plant life. Noddies and terns have protected nesting sites here and if you are very lucky you might spot the endemic Maria Islands ground lizard *(zandolite)*, a colourful but rarely seen creature, and the non-poisonous kouwess grass snake *(dromicus ornatus)*.

*Below: iguana country*
*Bottom: the Savannes Bay Nature Reserve*

Map on pages 58–9

*Below: divers are drawn by St Lucia's rich marine life*
*Bottom: Savannes Bay mangroves*

Access to the nature reserve is restricted to guided tours run by the St Lucia National Trust and to reach it from Vieux Fort visitors will need to take a small boat that ferries passengers across the channel. A protected archaeological site once used by Amerindians, the islets are largely given over to the nature reserve but there is a small beach where visitors can enjoy a picnic and go swimming, snorkelling and diving offshore.

## SAVANNES BAY NATURE RESERVE

Back on the mainland, travelling north from Vieux Fort along the East Coast brings you to an area of mangrove swamp. The ★★ **Savannes Bay Nature Reserve** encompasses the second-largest mangrove swamp in St Lucia, the first being nearby **Mankoté Mangrove**, which lies a little further south on the coast. Mangrove swamps are areas of brackish water where salt and fresh water meet.

The entire island's biodiversity makes St Lucia a valuable resource for environmentalists, while other visitors can gain access, albeit restricted, to sites such as Savannes Bay within an eco-system that remains virtually untouched by man. An extensive reef system runs from near the Maria Islands to the north end of the Savannes reserve, making snorkelling and diving along this section of the southeastern coast a popular attraction. Visitors also come here for the fishing and the wide variety of bird life that inhabits the rich mangrove swamp.

## MILITARY PROTECTION

Until the 1960s the Mankoté Mangrove and forest was used as a US military base, which, due to restricted access to the land, meant that the mangrove swamp suffered little or no damage caused by development elsewhere. However, once the US vacated the land, the swamp was opened up to commercial fishermen and hunters, until it was granted reserve status.

Nearby **Scorpion Island**, lying in the Savannes Bay, also contains red and black mangroves.

# Excursion: East Coast side trip

**Vieux Fort – Mamiku Gardens – Praslin – Fregate Islands Nature Reserve – Dennery**

This route is approached via Vieux Fort, but it can just as easily be attempted from Castries in the north and from the West Coast.

## THE WINDWARD SIDE

The East Coast road from Vieux Fort is well made and takes travellers on a scenic route past rugged coastline along the windward side of the island. This is the less commercial part of St Lucia with fewer large resorts and hotels than on the West Coast, but with a wealth of gardens, nature reserves, walking trails through the rainforest and small fishing hamlets. East Coast beaches are the nesting sites for leatherback, hawksbill and green turtles; the white-breasted thrasher and St Lucia wren have also been spotted here.

Around 16 km (9 miles) from Vieux Fort is **Micoud**, a small coastal village where, along with many other sites in the area, evidence of Amerindian settlement has been discovered.

The East Coast road crosses over the Troumassée River that skirts the edge of the fishing village and bypasses it on its west side. Clear signs direct drivers into Micoud proper, which is 6 km

Map on pages 58–9

**Micoud Celebrations**
John Compton, St Lucia's first prime minister in 1979, was Micoud's MP for over 25 years.

The village is an ideal place to visit during two of the island's biggest religious festivals, La Rose in August and La Marguerite in October. They are both celebrated with church services, street parades, lots of delicious food and a series of fun events.

*Explore the rainforest*

Map
on pages
58–9

(4 miles) east of the rainforest. The village is the starting and ending point for hikers attempting the walking trail that runs across the island through the **Quilesse Forest** and **Edmund Forest** reserves to **Fond St Jacques**, just outside Soufrière.

## MAMIKU GARDENS

West of Micoud and north of the Troumassée River is **Latille Waterfall** (entrance fee), which has 6-m (20-ft) cascades that descend into a pool below; bring your swimsuit and you can take a refreshing dip in the water.

Driving north from Micoud the road heads inland, passing places imaginatively and poignantly named Malgrétoute, Patience and Mon Repos. ★★★ **Mamiku Gardens** (daily 9am–5pm; tel: 455 3729; entrance fee) has 5 ha (12 acres) of grounds surrounding an old estate house. It is located off the main road less than 1 km north of Mon Repos in the Micoud Quarter, not far from Praslin Bay. In the 18th century Mamiku Estate was home to a French governor of the island; it later became a British military outpost during the tussle for ownership. By the early 20th century, it had fallen into a state of neglect and the owners transformed it into a banana plantation. It remains a working plantation.

## TROPICAL TREATS

Visitors to the colourful tropical gardens can explore the estate along a series of self-guided walking trails lined with delicate orchids, bright heliconia and fragile hibiscus and shaded by tall leafy trees, including the gommier, which is still used to make dug-out canoes by local boat builders. One of the trails leads a little way into the forest nearby. A small herb garden includes roots and plants used in bush medicine introduced to the island by enslaved West Africans. Also on the site are ruins and archaeological artefacts. Plenty of parking space is provided out front and the ticket booth has maps of the walking trails. Mamiku has a snack bar and a gift shop at the garden entrance.

*Walking the rainforest trails can be tricky*

## PRASLIN BAY AND ISLAND

★★★**Praslin Bay** lies opposite the two Fregate Islands and is fringed by red mangroves that front 5 ha (13 acres) of natural landscape. This is also part of the Fregate Islands Nature Reserve, which is managed by the St Lucia National Trust, in conjunction with a Praslin community project. Visitors may find more than 30 species of bird here and on the islands such as the St Lucian oriole, the great white heron and the red-billed tropic bird. The mature trees are the habitat of the harmless endemic boa constrictor *(constrictor constrictor orphics)*, which can grow to over 3.5 m (12 ft). There is a small interpretation centre on the peninsula.

Beyond the mangroves and dry forest is a cave network with evidence of an Amerindian settlement. Petroglyphs and remnants of ceramics and tools have been discovered along these parts.

The village of Praslin maintains the fishing tradition on which it was established and local boat builders construct fishing canoes from gommier trees using ancient techniques thought to have come from the first Amerindian settlers.

In the centre of Praslin Bay sits tiny ★★**Praslin Island**, a good place to watch the birdlife. You may see a St Lucian whiptail, which was introduced to the tiny island in 1995. Accessible by boat, the island is limited to 50 visitors at one time.

**Star Attractions**
● **Mamiku Gardens**
● **Praslin Bay**

*Bright orchids, beehive ginger and passionflowers decorate the island*

Map
on pages
58–9

# FREGATE ISLANDS NATURE RESERVE

Just off the East Coast north of Praslin Bay is the ★★★ **Fregate Islands Nature Reserve** (open year round; guided tours by appointment; tel: 455 3099 or 453 7656; email: fregate25@hotmail.com), which looks like a collection of rocks jutting out of the sea just a few steps away from the mainland. The two small islands that form the reserve, **Fregate Island Major** and **Fregate Island Minor**, have a combined size of less than half an hectare (1 acre). The largest of the two, Fregate Island Major, is inaccessible. A visit to the reserve entails a 1.6 km (1 mile) guided walk from Praslin village, which follows a loop trail cut along the cliff top on a mainland peninsula, allowing you to observe the wildlife on the islands just offshore. The walk takes approximately 1 hour 15 minutes to complete, so bring sturdy walking shoes and a hat for shade. Visitors are not encouraged to visit Fregate Island Minor, although it is possible to do so, because of the damage it may cause to the fragile environment.

The islands that are named after the frigate bird (*fregata magnificens*), which nests and roosts here, comprise mostly xerophytic vegetation, cacti, mangrove forest and open grass areas. Unfortunately the number of frigate birds that migrate to this spot from Cape Verde in Africa has dropped dramatically in recent years.

*Below: an Amerindian petroglyph*
*Bottom: juvenile frigate birds gather together*

## DENNERY BAY LOOKOUT

From Praslin Bay the East Coast road continues north, following the coastline and allowing travellers wonderful views of the rugged cliffs and the small villages that nestle on the hillside and near the beaches. A few miles north you come to **Dennery**, a medium-sized, but growing, town where many of the residents earn their living from the land or sea.

Just before the turn off into the town there is a viewpoint from where you can look out over **Dennery Bay** fronted by the expanding community. Leaving the town from the north, the road turns west and inland and climbs towards the interior through dry forest, passing Grande Rivière. From here travellers can head back to Castries in the north.

**Star Attraction**
● Fregate Islands
Nature Reserve

**Preserve and Protect**
The St Lucia National Trust has managed the Fregate Islands and nearby forest area since 1989, when the land was awarded reserve status.

## FOND D'OR BAY

About 1.6 km (1 mile) from Dennery, where the main road turns west into the Mabouya Valley, is **Fond D'Or Bay**. This crescent-shaped bay has a beach of white sand, backed by high sheer cliffs and a rugged landscape that is typical of the eastern Atlantic coast. Swimming is not recommended here because of the rough sea conditions, but the beach is worth a visit.

Driving from Dennery the view of the bay from the roadside lookout point is spectacular. Nearby, an old fort and plantation ruins have been developed as **Fond D'Or Nature Reserve and Historical Park** (daily; entrance fee; tel: 453 3242), with a wooded canopy of coconut palms, an estuarine forest and mangrove wetlands. Visitors can hike along the trails that weave through the forest and take a tour of the estate that contains the remnants of the sugar mill, windmill and the old planter's house, which has been transformed in to an interpretation centre. From one of the trails on the edge of the estate, walkers might spot the hill known locally as **Mabouya** or **La Sorcière** (the sorceress), which stands almost 7 km (4 miles) away in the Castries Waterworks Forest Reserve.

*Dennery is an expanding community*

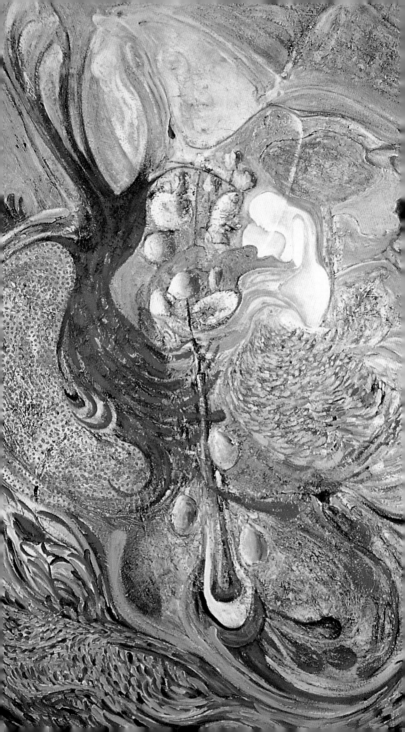

# Creole culture

St Lucia has a fascinating and complex culture
steeped in the history and tradition of other lands.
Like its highly seasoned Creole cuisine, the island
and its people have created a virtual pepperpot
culture, initially influenced by French and British
colonists and enslaved Africans, that has become
distinctively St Lucian. Today it is revealed in the
melodic Kwéyòl language, the colourful art and
literature, the festivals and music. The work of
playwright and theatre director Roderick Walcott,
writers such as Derek Walcott, Allan Weekes,
Michael Aubertin and Gandolph St Clair, Hunter
François, Charles Cadet, Stanley French, George
Alphonse, Melania Daniel and Ras Isley along
with artists Dunstan St Omer, Elwin Devaux, Vir-
ginia Henry and Corine George, and the folklorist
and historian Harold Simmons are but a few exam-
ples of the depth of the island's artistic output.

## LITERATURE

It is a wonder that such a tiny island has produced
so many artists of note, who reveal much about
the beauty of the language, landscapes and people through St Lucia's rich literary tradition.
Caribbean people have always had an oral tradition, for centuries stories, tall tales and proverbs
were passed on by word of mouth.

Before the 20th century Caribbean people were
more often written about than doing the writing
themselves, but that is no longer so. In fact this
island is the birthplace of Nobel Laureate, Derek
Walcott. Born in 1930, his father was a civil ser-
vant who was also a talented watercolourist and
his mother a respected headteacher. A poet, playwright, novelist and painter, Walcott, came to
prominence in the 1970s, but he actually began
writing in his youth, as can be seen by his *Collected Poems 1948–1984*. In 1990 his St Lucian
reworking of the Homeric legend in the poetic
epic, *Omeros*, firmly established him as one of
the world's greatest poets. In 1992 Walcott was
awarded the Nobel Prize for Literature. One of

**Bursting bamboo**
A familiar sound at Christmas time in the rural hill
areas, is the loud crack of bamboo
bursting. Traditionally young men
hollow out a piece of bamboo, insert
a stick and plug the bamboo with a
kerosene-soaked rag. When lit the
noise of the bamboo bursting can be
heard far away. Another Christmas
tradition is the equivalent of carol
singers, who sing Creole songs to
music from a *chack chack* band.

*Above: Derek Walcott*
*Opposite: Llewellyn Xavier's art*

Walcott's best-known plays, *Dream on Monkey Mountain* (1970), has entertained audiences throughout the Caribbean, North America and the UK over the years. Some of Walcott's stories and poems use motifs and imagery from the little fishing hamlets that he was familiar with as a boy, such as Soufrière and Gros Islet.

## FOLKLORE

St Lucian folktales heralding from as far back as slavery times have survived to the present day, such as the *Tim Tim* tales, which are still told today by a *kontè* or narrator. The stories of St Lucia have common elements found in tales from Africa and the rest of the Caribbean region, often only the names of the central characters have been changed. The island has a wealth of stories, riddles and proverbs about characters such as Konpè Lapin (rabbit), Konpè Makak (monkey), Konpè Chyen (dog) and Konpè Tig (tiger). While in other parts of the Caribbean you can hear similar tales about the trickster Anancy the spider.

*Below: carnival costumes are works of art*

Today St Lucians recognise the value of their heritage through folktales and traditions, which are being preserved and revived before they die out with their purveyors. Characters such as the Toes, Papa Jab and his followers can be seen in masquerades at Christmas and New Year. The work of the Folk Research Centre has made an impact; it maintains an important historical archive, runs workshops for school children, organises national festivals and events and has a theatre company that performs in Kwéyòl. Also influential is Marie 'Sessenne' Descartes whose songs preserve St Lucian folk culture.

## ART

Not only is the uniqueness of St Lucia expressed through its literature but also in its art such as that produced by Dunstan St Omer. His work can be seen displayed in public spaces all over the island, including religious artwork in the Capital's city cathedral and over the altar at the tiny church in

Jacmel. Several of St Omer's children are also artists, who have collaborated with their father at some time.

Llewellyn Xavier is an internationally recognised artist and an active environmentalist, his abstract works, oil on canvas, are a dazzling array of colour and texture often using Caribbean motifs reminiscent of the St Lucian landscape. He also produces original art using recycled materials. Xavier's work can be seen in collections in North America, the Caribbean and Europe *(see page 88)*.

Although St Lucia has no national gallery, exhibitions of the work of local artists are mounted regularly. A selection of commercial galleries include:

**Artsibit Gallery**, corner of Brazil and Mongiraud streets, tel: 452 7865.

**Fine Art Gallery**, Pointe Seraphine, Castries, tel: 459 0891. Commercial gallery exhibits the work of Llewellyn Xavier and other local and international artists.

**Llewellyn Xavier Studio**, Mount Du Cap, Cap Estate, tel: 450 9155. Showcase for the work of Llewellyn Xavier: oil abstracts and art from recycled products. View by appointment only.

**Modern Art Gallery**, Gros Islet Highway, Bois d'Orange, tel: 452 9079. Displays of contemporary Caribbean art.

**Snooty Agouti**, Rodney Bay, tel: 452 0321. A

**Cricket**
The official cricket season runs from January to July when there are inter-island matches and the regional West Indies team competes with other cricket-playing nations. Although St Lucia is yet to produce a world class Test cricketer the sport remains popular. There is an impressive 12,000-seat national cricket ground in Beausejour, which will be the venue for some of the Cricket World Cup matches in 2007.

*Below: music in art*

selection of Caribbean-originated woodcarvings, art and prints.

## CRAFTS

The African influence is best seen through the crafts and art produced on the island, particularly the woodcarvings of the island's craftsmen. Art in wood, of varying quality and size, can be found in artists studios, markets and souvenir shops all over St Lucia.

Choiseul is well-known for its distinctive clay pottery but here too artisans fashion fine hand-woven baskets that are sturdy enough to take to market and aesthetically pleasing enough for an excursion to the beach. The craft centre at La Fargue in southwest St Lucia showcases the work of potters, basket-weavers and wood-carvers, who continue crafts handed down from generation to generation.

Sculptor and woodcarver Vincent Joseph Eudovic works at his Goodlands studio in the hills of Morne Fortune. His beautiful abstract carvings are created from local woods such as laurier mabouey, teak, mahogany and red and white cedar. The ancient Indonesian art of batik is being preserved and given a Caribbean flavour at Caribelle Batik. Fabric is printed with bright colourful images taken straight from St Lucian wildlife and natural landscapes.

*The St Lucia Jazz Festival draws the crowds in May*

# FESTIVALS

St Lucians love to 'jump-up' (dance in the street) and there is no better time to visit than during one of the island's festivals. The St Lucia Jazz Festival draws an international crowd in May. But it is at Carnival time in July, on Jounen Kwéyòl Entenasyonnal (International Creole Day) in October and during the prominent festivals such as La Rose and La Marguerite that St Lucia's complex and colourful culture is truly revealed.

*Carnival time*

## CALENDAR OF EVENTS

| | |
|---|---|
| January 1 | New Year's Day |
| February 22 | Independence day |
| March/April | Easter Sunday (variable) |
| May 1 | Labour Day |
| | St Lucia Jazz Festival (variable) |
| July | Carnival (variable) |
| August 1 | Emancipation Day |
| August 30 | Feast of St Rose De Lima (La Rose) |
| October | Thanksgiving Day (first Monday) |
| October 17 | Feast of La Marguerite |
| October 31 | Jounen Kwéyòl Entenasyonnal |
| December | Atlantic Rally for Cruisers (variable) |
| December 13 | National Day |
| December 25 | Christmas Day |

# MUSIC

The rhythms and beats of St Lucian music reflects the energy and creativity of the people. Wherever you go on the island you will be entertained by the strains of folk music, cadence, zouk, calypso, steel pan, soca and reggae, country and western and highly influential US soul and R&B.

Folk songs by Marie 'Sessenne' Descartes, and Charles Cadet, the work of Ronald 'Boo' Hinkson and local calypsonians keep the oral tradition alive. In the bars and hotels you are more likely to hear reggae and soca than traditional folk music. But cadence and zouk, with their origins in French and African rhythms, and calypso songs in Kwéyòl are still performed by artists today and remain popular here and on other French Creole-speaking islands such as neighbouring Martinique and Dominica.

# FOOD AND DRINK

In almost every aspect of St Lucian culture there is a colourful blend of African, Amerindian, French and British influences, and nowhere more so than in its cuisine. The tropical climate and rich fertile soil mean that the island enjoys a near endless bounty of nature from cassava, sweet potato and dasheen to fragrant nutmeg, cinnamon and ginger. The landscape is punctuated with rich farmland where bananas, pineapple, grapefruit, oranges and mangoes grow in abundance. There is also superb seafood from the surrounding Caribbean Sea and the Atlantic Ocean,

Seafood has a distinct and intense flavour here, most likely because it is served so fresh. A rich source of protein, fish such as snapper, mahi mahi (also known as dorado or dolphin), wahoo, flying fish and tuna grace St Lucian plates. Here too you will find plenty of crab, spiny lobster (in season 1 September to 30 April) and conch. The result is that mealtimes can be a delicious cornucopia of fragrances and flavours.

## LOCAL SPECIALITIES

Many of the foods the Amerindian settlers grew and consumed are still around today, notably cassava, potatoes, sweet potatoes, yam, maize, peppers, okra, peanuts, cashew nuts, and pumpkin. The Amerindians delighted in roasted corn, and today it remains a popular and healthy snack. The island's street vendors roast the corn on barbecues, often until it is black.

Cassava bread is a St Lucian staple. First enjoyed by the Amerindians and later the enslaved West Africans brought with them their own version of the bread. Served as an accompaniment to a main meal or as a filling snack, modern cassava bread comes in a variety of flavours from sweet or cherry to smoked herring.

The island's national dish is green fig and salt fish, a tasty meal of seasoned salt cod and small green bananas, known locally as a fig. Also worth a try is hearty pumpkin soup or callaloo soup made from the green leaf of the dasheen, a common root vegetable. The leaves have a spinach-like appearance and can also be cooked up with onions and salt fish.

Salt fish was first introduced to the Caribbean as an easy-to-store, inexpensive source of protein for the slaves working the land and it was they who created imaginative ways to cook it. Making the best of what was on offer and what they could afford has inspired generations of Caribbean cooks, little wonder that menus include dishes made from almost every imaginable part of a pig or cow.

Pigs' tails are a local speciality, cooked in a juicy stew. Other stews include pepperpot – a combination of meats, vegetables and hot peppers with cassava juice – while souse bouillon contains salt beef cooked with a spicy mix of onions, beans, little dumplings and potatoes. Then there is cowheel soup and oxtail, chicken and beef, stewed, fried, baked or in mouthwatering curries.

Side dishes include breadfruit roasted, cut in slices or cubed in a salad; accras (fish cakes or bakes), cassava, dasheen, sweet potato, yam, green fig, plantain, lentils, plain rice and rice and peas, with one of several kinds of peas including green or dried pigeon peas, black eye, split peas or lentils. Reflecting an Indian influence is roti, a flat unleavened bread wrap that is a popular accompaniment to spicy meat dishes.

The food is flavoursome because of the seasonings used: most commonly onions, garlic, lime, peppers, thyme, ginger, clove, cinammon and nutmeg. You will find a bottle of hot pepper sauce – made from scotch bonnet pepper – on almost every table, but be careful as the strength of the sauce varies from mild to fiery. Another condiment with a distinctive flavour is banana ketchup, made from a secret blend of banana, herbs and spices.

## FRUIT BASKET

Well-known for its small sweet bananas, the island also produces a variety of tropical fruits including guava, soursop, mango *(see page 97)*, papaya (pronounced paw paw), pineapple, passionfruit, tamarind and coconut. Fruit is everywhere, made in to juice, ice cream, a pickle or chutney.

## SWEETS AND PASTRIES

The region's love affair with sugar stems back to the 17th-century plantation era when St Lucia began its relatively short-lived sugar industry. Those with a sweet tooth won't be disappointed with a choice of sweets

*Rum: good for cocktails or straight up.*

and pastries as different as tangy tamarind balls and coconut sugar cakes, cinnamon turnovers and banana bread. And don't forget the island fruit preserves such as guava jelly.

## WHAT TO DRINK

Refreshing fruit juices abound including orange, mango, pineapple, grapefruit, lime, guava and passionfruit.

Islanders are rightly proud of their rum. St Lucia Distillers produces a selection of dark and white rums at its factory in the Roseau Valley *(see page 55)*. The dark rums include Bounty, Buccaneer and an overproof favourite, Denros. Connoisseurs can try Old Fort Reserve, Admiral Rodney and Chairman's Reserve. Crystal is a white rum.

In the island rum shops (known as *cabawe*) rum is drunk straight up or on the rocks, but the uninitiated can enjoy theirs in a blend of tropical fruit juices. There are also ready-made rum punches such as Kwèyòl Spiced Rum or Smugglers rum punch, and rum-based liquers such as Crème a Caye, Orange Bliss and Koko-Nut rum. Less potent is local Piton lager or shandy, with an interesting twist of sorrel or ginger.

# Restaurants

Below is a selection of restaurants, divided into three categories: $$$ = expensive, $$ = moderate, $ = inexpensive.

## Castries

**Auberge Seraphine Restaurant**, Vigie Marina, tel: 453 2073. A lovely place with an international menu. Overlooks the marina. $$–$$$

**The Coal Pot**, Vigie Marina, tel: 452 5566. French cuisine with a Caribbean twist. Open Mon–Fri for lunch and dinner; Sat dinner only. $$

**The Green Parrot Restaurant**, Morne Fortune, tel: 452 3399. A well-established restaurant with a European and Caribbean menu and a well-deserved reputation. Tasty food in generous portions. Open daily 7am–midnight. $$–$$$

**Spinnakers Beach Bar and Grill**, St Lucia Yacht Club, Reduit Beach, tel: 452 8491. Open for breakfast, lunch and dinner. Creole fish, chicken, burgers and fries and daily specials. Close to the beach; showers and sun loungers can be rented. $

## Rodney Bay and North

**Buzz Seafood and Grill**, tel: 458 0450. Excellent seafood and steaks with an international flavour. Imaginative local dishes too such as lobster ravioli. Extensive wine list. Open daily for dinner and Sunday brunch. $$–$$$

**The Great House**, Cap Estate, tel: 450 0450. The restaurant, on the site of Cap Estate's original plantation house, has delicious French-Creole food, served in an elegant setting, with views of the sea. Tea is served 4.30–5.30pm. Closed Mon. $$–$$$

**Jambe de Bois**, Pigeon Island National Landmark, tel: 452 0321. Seafront cafe serving tasty St Lucian specialities in the park. $

**Key Largo**, Rodney Heights, tel: 452

> **Fragrant Fruit**
> Although there are more than 100 varieties of mango just seven can be found in great numbers on the island of St Lucia. Around 2,000 tons of the fruit are exported each year to as far afield as the UK. Of the seven common varieties only a few actually originate from St Lucia, they include the large juicy Cabishe, the Long and the Pa Louis mangoes. The sweet, orange-coloured Julie mango actually heralds from Trinidad. Though closely associated with the region the mango, like the banana, is not indigenous. The fruit, be it sweet or tart, smooth or stringy in texture, can be juiced to produce a drink, or made into ice cream or chutney.

0282. The ideal eatery for authentic Italian pizza, baked in a traditional wood fire oven; pasta too. $–$$

**The Lime**, near Reduit Beach, tel: 452 0761. Casual restaurant and bar serving generous portions of local specialities such as breadfruit salad, spicy lentils, jerk chicken, roti, plus a rotating meat and vegetarian dish of the day; good value cocktails, local lager and spirits. Eat in or take away. $–$$

**The Oriental Restaurant**, at the Rex St Lucian Resort, tel: 452 8351. Elegant and stylish hotel restaurant with Far Eastern-inspired cuisine. $$$

**Spices**, at the Bay Gardens Hotel, Rodney Bay, tel: 452 8060. A popular hotel restaurant that attracts local people and visitors alike. A La Carte menu makes good use of fresh local produce. Caribbean buffet on Wed; barbecue Sat night and lunch buffet Sun. $–$$

**Tilly's 2x4 Restaurant and Bar**, Gros Islet Highway, Rodney Heights, tel: 458 4440. Wooden Caribbean-style restaurant with a *cabawe* (rumshop). Informal dining on the balcony. Seafood, pork, callaloo soup, accras and the national dish of saltfish and green fig. $–$$

> **Small but sweet**
> Bananas grown in St Lucia and its neighbours in the Windward Islands are smaller and (some say) sweeter than the larger fruit from elsewhere. The island is closely associated with the banana, a dominant crop for decades until the late 1990s *(see page 15)*, when farmers were forced to begin diversifying crops. The plant takes 9–10 months to develop, and can propagate itself by producing suckers on its stem, which can be planted to produce another plant.

**Triangle**, near Reduit Beach. Basic with a choice of daily specials and large portions. Eat in or take away. $

## Marigot Bay

**Chateau Mygo**, Marigot Bay, tel: 451 4772. Creole specialities with an East Indian twist; local vegetables, flying fish and mahi mahi. $$–$$$

**Doolittle's**, Marigot Beach Club, tel: 451 4974. Casual, elegant oceanside dining with a Creole-European menu including pumpkin soup, spicy chicken roti, beef pepperpot stew and fresh fish. Happy hour 5–7pm; live entertainment Tues, Wed, Thurs, Sat and Sun nights. $$$

**JJ's Paradise**, at JJ's Paradise Resort, tel: 451 4076. Local specialities in a lovely setting overlooking Marigot Bay. Very busy on Wed night – crab night. Delicious Creole crab, shrimp and lobster in season; meat dishes too. Happy hour 5–7pm. $–$$

## Soufrière and Environs

**Dasheene**, at Ladera Resort, tel: 459 7323. A stylish, elegant restaurant that has innovative dishes using the freshest local ingredients. Breathtaking views of the Pitons and out to sea. Expensive but well worth it. $$$

**La Haut Plantation**, West Coast Road, Soufrière, tel: 459 7008. Tasty international and Creole-influenced cuisine including fresh conch and spicy shrimp. Set in a hillside on the way to Soufrière. $$–$$$

**The Mango Tree Restaurant and Bar**, Stonefield Estate, Soufrière, tel: 459 7586. On the hillside with views to Petit Piton. Relaxed atmosphere with tasty local dishes such as spicy roti; good choice for a snack or main meal. Barbecue on Thurs. Open daily 7.30am–10pm. $$–$$$

**The Old Courthouse Restaurant**, Soufrière, tel: 459 5002. On the waterfront with views along the pier. The menu is French-Creole with lots of seafood in a variety of incarnations such as Creole calamari. $

**Plas Kassav**, Anse La Verdue, Canaries, tel: 459 4050. Roadside cafe-bakery with fresh-baked cassava bread in a choice of flavours. $

## Vieux Fort and South Coast

**The Reef Beach Cafe**, Anse De Sables, tel: 454 3418. Casual beach cafe with Caribbean fare including salt fish and bakes, seafood salad and T-bone steak; burgers and fries. Internet access and wheelchair access. $

## East Coast

**Whispering Palm**, at the Fox Grove Inn, Mon Repos, tel: 455 3271. A fine restaurant with views of Praslin Bay and the Fregate Islands. International menu with mussels, tuna and steak. Open daily for breakfast, lunch, and dinner. $$–$$$

## Fast Food

St Lucia has fast food outlets selling pizza, fried chicken and Caribbean snacks. Good for pizza are **Pizza Pizza** (tel: 452 8115) and **Domino's Pizza** (458 0002) in Rodney Bay. There are also a handful of **Kentucky Fried Chicken** outlets, in Castries, Rodney Bay and Vieux Fort.

## NIGHTLIFE

Many restaurants and bars have live music where you can while away the hours and there are nightclubs where you can shed calories on the dance floor. In Soufrière at the Jalousie Hilton Resort is **Bang Between the Pitons** (tel: 459 7864) a restaurant and rum shop. Rodney Bay has an array of entertainment including **Cinema 2000** (tel: 452 8802), showing first-run movies. Nightspots include **Indies** (tel: 452 0727), which is used mainly as a function and concert venue; the **Jazz Lounge** (tel: 458 0565) at the Roof Garden Restaurant on Seagrape Avenue with live late- night jazz five nights per week from 11pm; and **Shamrock's Pub** (tel: 452 8725), a lively Irish bar, down the road from the Rex St Lucian Resort, which is popular at the weekend. Nearby **The Lime** (tel: 452 0761), near Reduit Beach, is a casual hangout with a sports bar and karaoke nights. Caribbean and international artists perform at the **Gaiety** (tel: 450 0186), a large concert venue between Gros Islet and Pigeon Island. St Lucia Jazz Festival events are also held here.

The **Friday Night Jump-up** *(see page 40)* at Gros Islet is fun, but remember that things don't hot up until after 10pm. Street vendors and restaurants provide food, so there's no need to go hungry. Try barbecue chicken or fried fish and bakes washed down with an ice cold Piton lager. The event has a real party atmosphere and few people can resist the temptation to 'jump-up' and dance – the rhythms and beats from the sound systems that set up on the street are infectious.

**Seafood Friday** *(see page 57)* at Anse La Raye is a more tame and earlier evening fish fry. Tables are laid out for diners and loud reggae, calypso and kaiso music is pumped out of the bars. Most hotels organise an evening excursion to one or both fish fries and local guides will escort you too.

In May the **St Lucia Jazz Festival** sweeps across the island. It has an impressive line-up of international jazz and R&B artists and hosts day and evening events at venues everywhere, including Derek Walcott Square in Castries, Rodney Bay, Pigeon Island National Landmark and Derek Walcott Theatre at the Great House Restaurant. For more information visit www.stluciajazz.org.

*Friday Night Jump-up at Gros Islet.*

# ACTIVE HOLIDAYS

## WATER SPORTS
### Diving

The coast of St Lucia is blessed with the warm water of the Caribbean Sea, with an average temperature of 24°C (75°F) and is the ideal place to scuba dive. Experienced divers can enjoy rich, colourful marine life just a few yards from the beach in some cases, while beginners can take to the water confidently with an expert instructor. The water here is home to angel fish and sea horses, octopus and turtles, black coral and spectacular sponges. The natural reefs are pristine and several shipwrecks around the coast provide fascinating artificial reefs.

Some of the island's most beautiful dive sites are located in protected marine areas such as the Soufrière Marine Management Area (SMMA), which extends from Anse Jambon to Anse L'Ivrogne near Gros Piton on the West Coast *(see page 66)*. The rise of tourism and its pollutant consequences and the need to maintain the fishing stock led the government to attempt to

*Water sports at Hummingbird Beach*

protect the fragile reefs in particular and the island's ecosystem in general.

The result is that St Lucia has become a popular Caribbean dive destination. In just a few days visitors can qualify as a certificated PADI or NAUI diver and experience the wonders of the deep.

On the West Coast near Soufrière are several excellent dive sites. **Anse Chastanet Reef** attracts novices and experienced divers. The marine life is just a short walk in the water from the volcanic sand beach, and there are caves to explore in the relatively shallow parts. Experienced divers can enjoy **Fairyland**, an interesting drift dive that can be affected by the area's strong currents. Here too is the Anse Chastanet resort and the base of Scuba St Lucia, which also has facilities for snorkellers.

Just outside Soufrière Bay is an exciting dive site known as **Key Hole Pinnacles** – four tall gorgonians that stand several hundred feet high but remain below the water.

**Anse La Raye** has a reef just off the beach and is believed by some to have

the island's best wall and drift dives. Wreck divers are also catered for here. An artificial reef has been created by the deliberate sinking of an old 50-metre (165-ft) freighter, the *Lesleen M*. The coral encrusted wreck, which stands in 18 metres (60ft) of water is overrun with colourful fish and is located near Anse Cochon and Anse La Raye.

Don't forget to bring your dive certificate because you will not be allowed to rent equipment and dive unless you can prove your competence. There are plenty of accredited dive centres on the island, which can provide thorough instruction and the opportunity to explore some of the best dive sites in the Caribbean. A small selection of dive centres, which also have dive shops, are listed below:

**Dive Fair Helen**, Ciceron, PO Box MF 7071, tel: 451 7716, email: sam@divefairhelen.com www.divefairhelen.com

**Frog's Diving**, Harmony Suites, Rodney Bay, tel: 450 8831/458 0798, email: tee-j@candw.lc www.frogsdiving.com

**Marigot Beach Club Hotel & Dive Resort**, Marigot Bay PO, Castries, St Lucia, tel: 451 4974, email: mbc@candw.lc www.marigotdiveresort.com

**Scuba St Lucia**, Anse Chastanet Resort, PO Box 7000, Soufrière, St Lucia, tel: 459 7755, email: ansechastanet@candw.lc. www.scubastlucia.com

## Snorkelling

You don't have to be an accomplished diver to enjoy St Lucia's reef system. A guided snorkel tour can provide a fascinating insight into tropical marine life. The guide will identify the many different kinds of fish and coral and will rent out equipment, unless you prefer to bring your own.

**West Coast Marine Areas**
The West Coast of St Lucia has four main protected Marine Reserve Areas (MRAS) that require a permit to dive. They are Anse Chastanet, Rachette Pointe, Petit Piton and Gros Piton, which also has very limited access. Divers can apply for annual or daily permits, which are available from the Soufrière Marine Management Area (SMMA) office (tel: 459 5500) in Soufrière, or any authorised dive operator.

Snorkellers of all ages will find schools of colourful fish and other marine life around Anse Mamin, just north of Anse Chastanet and at Anse Cochon, south of Anse La Raye. North and south of Petit Piton, Malgretoute and Beausejour are also good for snorkelling. If you are snorkelling independently be sure to stay close to the beach and never underestimate the strength of the sea currents. Alternatively you can join a boat tour run by one of the island's dive operators.

## River and Coastal Kayaking

Explore the island's rainforests and shady mangrove swamps by water. Guided kayaking tours are an exciting way to see the dense forest areas and wildlife. There are tours along the Roseau River and the western coastline, departing from Anse Cochon, south of Anse La Raye and pitching up at Anse La Liberté *(see page 62)*. There are also kayaking trips around Pigeon Island National Landmark.

**Oasis Marigot**, Marigot Bay, tel: 451-4185, email: info@oasismarigot.com www.oasismarigot.com

## Windsurfing

The southern coast is a magnet for experienced and adventurous windsurfers who are attracted by the challenge of the strong winds that can whip

> ### Jungle Biking
> Cycling along the forest and planta-tion trails at Anse Mamin Plantation can be a hair-raising experience and an exciting way to explore. Ride through groves of tropical fruit trees heavy with banana, mango and cocoa or visit the 18th-century ruins on the estate. The trails maintained by Bike St Lucia vary in difficulty from yellow (lower inter-mediate), red (intermediate) to black (expert). The most challenging ride is Tinker's trail, that has a steep uphill and fast downhill track.

up the Atlantic waves off Anse de Sables at Vieux Fort. Cas-en-Bas in the northeast is also a popular spot. Wind-surf sails bobbing on the water are a sight to behold. Less experienced windsurfers may prefer the relatively quiet Caribbean Sea on the West Coast. The best time to windsurf is December to May when the trade winds are most consistent. However, you may still catch a good breeze in the summer.

Anse de Sables has pretty white sand with a cafe, public toilets and shower facilities. In contrast there are no facilities to speak of at Cas-en-Bas, in the island's far north and it can be difficult to reach by road, even with a four-wheel-drive.

Rent windsurf boards or take lessons at the water sports facilities of large hotels and resorts and also through dive operators.

**Club Mistral Windsurfing**, Anse de Sables Beach, Vieux Fort, St. Lucia, email: windsurf@slucia.com
www.slucia.com/windsurf

### Kitesurfing

A variation on windsurfing is kitesurf-ing, which also embraces elements of paragliding and traditional surfing. Supported by a kite, you can get a glimpse of St Lucia's rugged coastal landscape. You're practically fully equipped with a surfboard, a kite small enough to be stored in a backpack and a few lessons. Club Mistral can organ-ise kitesurfing instruction.

**Club Mistral Skyriders**, Anse de Sables, Vieux Fort, tel: 454 3327, email: skyriders@slucia.com

**Tornado Kite & Surf St Lucia**, Anse de Sables, tel: 454 7579/486 0545, email: office@tornado-surf.com
www.tornado-surf.com

### Fishing

The warm Caribbean waters are teem-ing with fish and, depending on the time of year, you could reel in big game fish such as marlin, wahoo, king-fish sailfish and dorado (mahi mahi); tuna and barracuda are known in these waters too. Deep sea or sport fishing is popular and every year there are numerous events and competitions attended by local and visiting fisher-men. The three-day St Lucia Bill Fishing Tournament is held in Sep-tember. Most operators follow a catch and release code.

Visitors can book a day of half-day fishing trip where they may also spot turtles, dolphins and whales in season.

**Captain Mike's Sport Fishing & Pleasure Cruises**, Vigie Marina, Castries, tel: 452 7044, email: capt.mikes@candw.lc
www.worldwidefishing.com/stlucia

**Hackshaws Boat Charter & Sport Fishing**, Vigie Marina, tel: 453 0553, email: hackshawc@candw.lc

**Mako Watersports**, Rodney Bay, tel: 452 0412, email: makowatersports@hotmail.com
www.stluciabusiness.com/mako.htm

**MISS T Charters**, Vigie Marina, tel: 459 0790/453 0553/584 2820, email: capt_ps44@yahoo.com

**Trivial Pursuit Charters**, Clarke Ave., Vigie, Castries, tel: 459 0780 (at Casa del Vega), email: sultina@hotmail.com
www.trivialpursuitfishingcharters.com

## Whale Watching

Whales are cetaceans, some of the largest mammals in the world. Here, around this tiny island, many species of resident and migratory whales can be seen in the warm Caribbean waters. The various species can be seen at different times of year, especially during the migratory mating season from October to April. Most common are sperm whales, pilot whales, humpback whales and false killer whales. Common, spinner, spotted, striped and bottlenose dolphins can also be spotted accompanying the whales, sometimes leaping high above the water.

**Captain Mike's Sport Fishing & Pleasure Cruises**, tel: 452 7044
**Hackshaws Boat Charter & Sport Fishing**, tel: 453 0553

## Sailing

An exciting way to explore the coast and see the scenic landscape is by boat. Boat tours can include a spot of diving, snorkelling, swimming or sport fishing, and can be day or sunset party cruises. Full- and half-day sails can be arranged through one of the local boat charter companies based at the marina at Castries, Rodney Bay Marina, Marigot Bay and Soufrière.

Depending on the time of year St Lucia hosts numerous sailing events, many of them beginning or ending at Rodney Bay Marina. The St Lucia Regatta is a five race series and the Atlantic Rally for Cruisers *(see page 39–40)* is an annual race event from the Canary Islands to St Lucia.

**St Lucia Yachting Association**, tel: 450 8651, email: catsltd@candw.lc
**Star Trek Charters**, Rodney Bay Marina, tel: 452 3430
**Endless Summer Cruises**, tel: 450 8651, email: catsltd@candw.lc, www.endlesssummer.net
**Mystic Man Tours**, Bay Street, Soufrière, tel: 459 7783, email: aimablec@candw.lc, www.mysticmantours.com
**The Brig** *Unicorn*, Rodney Bay Marina *(see page 29)*, tel: 452 8644, www.brigunicorn.com

## CYCLING

Tours by bike can be challenging but rewarding for visitors who want to get close to nature, since a bike can get to places a motor vehicle cannot. There are mountain bike trips through the interior, exploring the trails that run through the scenic countryside and

*Cycling around town*

dense beautiful forest, and stopping for a dip in a cooling waterfall. Trips from Rodney Bay to the far north provide an opportunity to view the spectacular rugged Atlantic coast, and to the Soufrière area too, with its banana plantations, Botanical Gardens and Sulphur Springs. Not for the faint hearted are the bike trails cut through lush vegetation on the Anse Mamin Plantation. Here Bike St Lucia has trails for the beginner and for the professional mountain biker.

**Bike St Lucia**, tel: 459 2453, email: bikestlucia@candw.lc www.bikestlucia.com

**Island Bike Hikes**, tel: 458 0908, email: mtnbikeslu@candw.lc www.cyclestlucia.com

## HIKING

Exploring the island interior on foot is one way to experience some of the breathtaking scenery that makes up the volcanic island's landscape. With almost year round warm sunshine and summer temperatures rising above 88°F (31°C) the high mountain and forest areas, where it is several degrees cooler, provide walkers with welcome relief from the heat.

St Lucia has 77 sq km (19,000 acres) of protected forest land, which is the natural habitat of rare plants, trees, birds and wildlife. As a result walking tours are permitted only with an official guide. Forest walks and hikes vary in difficulty.

### Rainforest Trails

The **Edmund Forest Reserve** in St Lucia's heartland can be approached from the west. The journey takes travellers through small country hamlets, along bumpy potholed roads and affords views of the magnificent Mount Gimie before finally reaching the forest area, the entrance of which has a manned ranger station and a

**Fregate Island Nature Reserve**
Tours of the Fregate Island Nature Reserve operate year round and can be arranged through Eastern Tours (tel: 455 3099/3152). The larger of the two Islands, Fregate Island Major is inaccessible but visitors can still see the nesting sites of the frigate birds, for which the islands are named, from the adjacent peninsula, which also forms part of the reserve. Here are more than 100 plant species, almost 40 bird species and rare wildlife.

public toilet. A three-hour hike along the reserve's strenuous walking trails leads deep into the forest, where you can enjoy the shade of tall ferns, blue mahoe, bamboo and mahogany laced with bromeliads, lianas and orchids. Here too are fabulous flora and fruit such as bird of paradise, bright heliconia and hibiscus, banana trees and pineapple plants.

Visitors need to be fit to attempt the 4-km (2½-mile) **Enbas Saut Forest Trail**, which takes walkers through hill country to two cascades of mountain fresh water that flow into clear pools below, and beyond to the Troumassée River and the hamlet of Micoud on the East Coast.

Nearby the lush canopied **Quilesse Forest Reserve** is the habitat of the rarely seen St Lucia Parrot (*Amazona versicolor*) known locally as jacquot. The walking trails through this reserve can also provide glimpses of other indigenous island wildlife.

The moderately taxing **Barre de L'Isle Trail** (1.6km/1-mile) cuts through the forest in an east to west direction and provides unforgettable panoramic views over the Cul-de-Sac and Mabouya valleys and out to the Atlantic Coast.

A short drive (30 minutes) southeast of Castries is the 5-km (3-mile) **Forestière Trail**. It follows an old

French road through a mature forest with lush ferns and fig trees.

In the forest heartland is the 3-km (1¼-mile) trail through the Millet Bird Sanctuary, with species of rare bird. For more information about the forest reserves and other national heritage sites or to book a trail hike contact:
**St Lucia Forestry Department**, tel: 450 2231/2078,
email: deptforest@slumaffe.org
www.slumaffe.org
**St Lucia Heritage Tours**, tel: 451 6058 (Pointe Seraphine); 451 5067 (La Place Carenage),
email: sluheritage@candw.lc
www.heritagetoursstlucia.com
**Trust Trek and Tours** (operated by the St Lucia National Trust), tel: 453 7656; 452 8735, email: natrust@candw.lc, www.slunatrust.org/tours

## BIRDWATCHING

With such vast forested areas and a mountain landscape, visitors to St Lucia can spot some of the region's colourful and rare, indigenous and migratory birds. With patience and luck you may see some wonderful tropical birds such as the endangered St Lucia wren (*Troglodytes aedon mesoleucus*), St Lucia black finch (*Melanospiza richardsoni*), the white breasted thrasher *(Ramphocinclus brachyurus sanctaeluciae)* and the national bird, the St Lucia parrot (*Amazona versicolor*), with a bright blue face, green wings and a red patch across the throat and chest.

Several forest areas throughout the island are especially good for birdwatching, including the Millet Bird Sanctuary, Edmund Forest Reserve, Quilesse Forest Reserve , Grand Anse, Grand Bois Forest, Fregate Islands Nature Reserve, Maria Islands Nature Reserve, Savannes Bay Nature Reserve and the Monkoté Mangrove swamp. Birdwatching tours can be arranged through the Forestry Department, tel: 450 2231/2078.

## HORSE RIDING

Touring the island forests, plantations and coastal landscapes on horseback can be fun. Choose from a scenic ride around the Morne Coubaril Estate and surrounding area, or along a picturesque Atlantic coast beach.
**International Pony Club**, Gros Islet, tel: 452 8139,
email: stefanof@candw.lc
**Morne Coubaril Estate**, Soufrière, tel: 459 7340
**Trim's National Riding**, Cas-en-Bas, Castries, tel: 450 8273,
email: trimsridingstables@candw.lc

## JEEP SAFARI & ATV TOURS

Island excursions by sturdy open-top jeep through the forest and rural hill areas is an exciting way to see St Lucia. And racing through plantation land on an all-terrain vehicle adds a touch of adventure to any trip.
**Jeep Safari**, tel: 452 0504,
email: jeepsafari@candw.lc
**ATV Adventures Ltd**, tel: 458 8280/1, email: mctours@candw.lc

## GOLF

There is a good 18-hole public golf course at Cap Estate in the far north of the island.
**St Lucia Golf and Country Club**, Rodney Bay, tel: 450 8523,
www.stluciagolf.com

## TENNIS

Most large resorts have tennis courts that can be rented by the hour, lessons can also be booked.
**Rex St Lucian Hotel**, Rodney Bay, tel: 452 8351, www.rexcaribbean.com. There are floodlit tennis courts available to guests and non-guests of the hotel.
**St Lucia Racquet Club**, Cap Estate, tel: 450 0106.

# PRACTICAL INFORMATION

## Getting There

### By Air

Several international carriers including British Airways, Virgin Atlantic, American Airlines, Air Canada and BWIA, serve St Lucia bringing passengers from the UK and Europe, the US and Canada. Other airlines that provide inter-island flights to the George F. L. Charles Airport in Castries include LIAT, Caribbean Star, BWIA, Air Martinique, Helenair and American Eagle.

### From the US

US Airways flies direct to St Lucia from Philadelphia at the weekend, while American Eagle has a daily service from Puerto Rico and BWIA has a weekly flight from Miami and New York. Air Jamaica operates weekly flights from New York.

### From the UK

Virgin has three weekly flights to Hewanorra International, one non-stop to the island and the other two are via

*Adventure by jeep*

Barbados. British Airways flies via Antigua twice a week and BWIA also has a twice-weekly service to St Lucia with a stopover in Barbados.

### From Canada

Air Canada operates direct weekly flights from Toronto and Montreal. Several airlines also have additional charter flights from London, UK, and Toronto during the busy winter season (November to March).

Most international passengers arrive at **Hewanorra International Airport** in Vieux Fort, 67 km (42 miles) from Castries. Some visitors from other Caribbean islands and the US can get a direct flight to **George F. L. Charles Airport** in Castries, which lies near the harbour. There is a shuttle from Hewanorra to Castries for those who don't want to make the long journey from the south to the West Coast by road.

Alternatively, you can transfer from the international airport by helicopter to Castries and a handful of West Coast hotels that have heli-pads such as the Jalousie Hilton. It's not a cheap

option but it does cut travelling time right down to less than 15 minutes for the trip from Hewanorra International Airport to George F.L. Charles Airport in Castries, whereas the same trip by road could take anything from 1½ to 2 hours. For more information about helicopter transfers contact:

**St Lucia Helicopters Ltd**, tel: 453 6952; 453 6950 (pager); fax: 452 1553; www.stluciahelicopters.com

## BY SEA
### Cruises

St Lucia is a popular port of call for cruise ships starting their southern routes from San Juan, Puerto Rico and Barbados. The port of entry is Pointe Seraphine in Castries and the view across the bay and along the West Coast as the ship approaches is stunning. Some ships will also sail south before heading out of St Lucian waters to allow passengers the breathtaking views of the Pitons and Soufrière.

## TOUR OPERATORS

**Caribtours**, tel: 020 7751 0660; www.caribtours.co.uk. Organises tailor-made holidays to the Caribbean.
**Sunset Faraway Holidays**, tel: 020 7498 9922; www.sunset.co.uk. Luxury holidays to the Caribbean; they will also arrange island weddings.

# Getting Around

## BY ROAD
### Buses

The public bus system in St Lucia operates from early in the morning until early evening. It is safe to say that more buses run in the morning but the frequency tends to tail off after the end of the working day. Of course the towns with the larger populations, such as Castries, Soufrière and Vieux Fort, have the best services, while the more remote rural areas aren't always

as well served. The routes are zoned and priced accordingly, so a short hop can cost EC$1–2, while a longer trip from Castries to Soufrière can cost up to EC$10; you must have the exact fare. The Castries bus terminus is behind the Central Market and in Soufrière the bus stand is at the town square, on Henry Belmar and Sir Arthur Lewis streets. If you do travel on the bus you will hear local people call out 'one stop' when they want to get off, why not go ahead and try it once you are familiar with the route, otherwise ask the driver to let you know when you reach your destination.

### Taxis

Taxis are available in the form of a saloon vehicle or a minivan that can accommodate a small group. They are plentiful at the airports, in the resort areas at hotels, at shopping malls and in town at the official stands. Taxis are not metered because fares are fixed and the majority of drivers tend to stick to the reasonable published rate. However, there are some unscrupulous drivers so check the fare first.

A taxi is the obvious choice for a hotel transfer to and from the airport, unless your hotel offers a shuttle service. You can also arrange for a taxi driver/guide to take you on an island tour, on a shopping trip, or on an excursion to the Friday Night fish fry at Anse La Raye and the Jump-up at Gros Islet. Some reliable and knowledgeable local drivers and taxi services include:

Ben's Taxi Service, on the West Coast, tel: 459 5457/7160;
email: saltibusb@slucia.com
Julian Bissette, tel: 284 5476; email: bissettejc@candw.lc
Macarinus Charlemagne, tel: 485 9213; email: TX1022@hotmail.com
Allan Sampson, tel: 452 2651.

## Car Rental

In St Lucia you drive on the left. Visiting drivers must be over 25 years old and should obtain a temporary driving permit, which is valid for three months, by presenting a current driving license at the main police station (Bridge Street, Castries), or the car rental company. There is a small charge of around EC$54 for the permit. Seat belts are compulsory.

There is a choice of car rental companies and several, such as Ben's West Coast Jeeps, will deliver the vehicle to your hotel and pick up at the end of the rental period.

**Avis**, tel: 451 6976; email: avisslu@candw.lc

**Ben's West Coast Jeeps and Taxi Service**, tel: 459 5457/7160; www.westcoastjeeps.com

**Alto**, tel: 452 0233; www.altorentacar.com

**Cool Breeze Jeep-Car Rental**, tel: 454 7898; www.coolbreezecarrental.com

**Hertz**, tel: 452 0680; www.hertz@candw.lc

## INTER-ISLAND LINKS

### Airlines

A handful of Caribbean operators, including Caribbean Star, LIAT, Carib Aviation and Air Caraïbes offer basic inter-island air transport throughout the Caribbean region.

**LIAT**, tel: 452 3051/2; email: reservations@liatairline.com; www.fly-liat.com

**BWIA**, tel: 452 3778; 1 800 538 2942; email: mail@bwee.com

**Caribbean Star Airlines**, tel: 453 2927/452 5898; 1 800 744 7827 (toll free in the Caribbean); email: slugsa@flycaribbeanstar.com; www.flycaribbeanstar.com

## FERRIES

The **L'Express des Iles** ferry is a high-speed catamaran service that runs between St Lucia, Martinique, Dominica and Guadeloupe. The ferry leaves from the wharf at Castries, near La Place Carenage.

There is a service from Castries to Fort de France, Martinique (1 hour 20 minutes), four times a week; to Dominica and Guadeloupe three times a week. Travelling time is short enough to justify hopping over to a neighbouring island for a day or even a weekend. For reservations contact Cox & Company Ltd, tel: 452 2211.

**Caribbean Ferries** has a fast catamaran service transporting passengers from St Lucia to Martinique in 50 minutes, twice a week. The ferry, which also goes to Guadeloupe and Dominica, accommodates foot passengers and cars. Book through Pitons Travel, tel: 450 1486/7 *(see page 109)*.

**Maritime Silver Line** operates a shuttle service between Rodney Bay Marina and Martinique. The 12-seater ferries are smaller and slower (1 hour 30 minutes) than the catamarans, but the cost of the journey is usually less expensive. Contact Compagnie Maritime Silver Line, tel: 458 3508.

**Windward Lines Ltd** operates a freight service between Venezuela, Trinidad, St Vincent, Barbados and St Lucia and will sometimes accept passengers at certain times of year. For more information about sailing dates and times contact Windward Agencies in Barbados, tel: (246) 425 7402.

### Etiquette

As in the Caribbean in general, good manners go a long way in St Lucia. "Please", "Thank you", and a respectful and friendly demeanour will go a long way. "Hello", "Goodbye", "Good Morning" and "Good night" are used in every arena be it your hotel, a local bar, restaurant and to strangers you pass on the road. If you need to ask directions or advice always greet the person before asking a question. Don't take anyone's picture without first asking permission and don't refer to island residents as "natives".

# Facts for the Visitor

## ENTRY REQUIREMENTS

Passports are required for entry to St Lucia, except for US, Canadian and some citizens of neighbouring islands that are members of the Organisation of Eastern Caribbean States (OECS), who can technically travel with proof of identity such as a birth certificate and a valid photo ID. However, re-entering the USA without a valid passport has become increasingly difficult, even for genuine US citizens. Entry regulations for the USA have been tightened up in recent years.

## CUSTOMS

It is prohibited to enter St Lucia with illegal drugs or firearms. Duty free allowances for travellers visiting the island are 200 cigarettes or 250 grams of tobacco and 1 litre of wine or spirits.

## TOURIST INFORMATION

The St Lucia Tourist Board has branches in the UK and North America where you can pick up brochures and information about the island. The Tourist Board's administrative office is in Castries, however there are satellite offices and information booths at Hewanorra and George F.L. Charles airports, Pointe Seraphine shopping mall in Castries, on Bay Street in Soufrière and in the main tourist centres.

## TOURIST BOARD OFFICE IN ST LUCIA

PO Box 221, Sureline Building, Vide Bouteille, Castries, tel: 452 4094; fax: 453 1121; www.stlucia.org

## TOURIST BOARD OFFICES ABROAD

**Canada**, 8 King St East, Suite 700, Toronto, Ontario M5C 1B5; tel: (416) 362 4242; fax: (416) 362 7832, email: sltbcanada@aol.com
**UK**, 1 Collingham Gardens, London SW5 0HW; tel: 0870 900 7697; fax: 020 7341 7001; email: sltbinfo@stluciauk.org
**USA**, 800 Second Avenue, 9th Floor, New York, NY 10017; tel: (212) 867 2951/2950; fax: (212) 867 2795; email: info@st-lucia.com

## GUIDED TOURS

**Barefoot Holidays**, Rodney Bay; tel: 450 0507; email: barefoot@candw.lc; www.barefootholidays.com
**Spice Travel**, Reduit; tel: 452 0865/6; email: thomm@candw.lc, casalucia@candw.lc; www.casalucia.com
**Pitons Travel**, Richard Fanis Building, Marisule, Castries; tel: 450 1486/7; www.pitonstravel.com
**St Lucia Reps/Sunlink Tours**, Reduit Beach Avenue, Rodney Bay; tel: 456 9100/1-800-SUNLINK; www.sunlinktours.com

## CURRENCY

The official currency of St Lucia is the Eastern Caribbean dollar (EC$), which is pegged to the US dollar. The US dollar and all major credit cards and travellers' cheques are also accepted in most places including restaurants and shops, especially in the resort areas.

EC dollars are produced in denominations of $100, $50, $20, $10 and $5 notes; $1, 25¢, 10¢, 5¢, 2¢ and 1¢ coins.

There are foreign exchange and banking facilities in Castries, Rodney Bay, Vieux Fort, Soufrière and at Hewanorra International Airport, which is usually open from 12.30pm until the last flight leaves.

## TIPPING

Be prepared to pay a 10 percent service charge and 8 percent government tax on all goods and services. In particular most restaurants and hotels will often automatically add a 10–15 percent service charge to your bill, so no further gratuity is necessary unless you would like to tip an especially attentive waiter or another member of staff. Where service is not included a tip of 10–20 percent is appropriate.

## BUSINESS HOURS

Banks are generally open Monday to Friday 8am–3pm, while the banks in Rodney Bay tend to also open on Saturday 8am–noon.

## PUBLIC HOLIDAYS

1 January: New Year's Day
2 January: New Year's Holiday
22 February: Independence Day
March/April (variable): Easter
1 May: Labour Day
1 August: Emancipation Day
30 August: Feast of St Rosa de Lima
17 October: Feast of La Marguérite
13 December: National Day
25 December: Christmas Day
26 December: Boxing Day

## POSTAL SERVICE

The main post office in Castries is located on Bridge Street; there you can

buy stamps and phonecards. There are also small post offices in most towns and generally they are open Monday to Friday 8.30am–4.30pm.

## TELEPHONE & COMMUNICATIONS

Calls home from your hotel can be prohibitively expensive so it is advisable to make calls from public payphones, if you have change, or a calling station where you can use pre-paid phonecards.

The Cable and Wireless office on Bridge Street in Castries, near the post office, has public telephones and sells a wide selection of phonecards.

Cellular phones can be rented from specialist suppliers and since services are being deregulated, calls may be less expensive in the future.

There are internet cafes and facilities throughout the island, in the resort areas and in shopping centres such as Gablewoods Mall, just outside the centre of Castries.

The international country code for St Lucia is **758**.

## TIME ZONE

Atlantic Standard Time: four hours behind Greenwich Mean Time.

*Shopping in Castries*

## MEDIA
### Print

St Lucia has six newspapers including *The Voice*, which is published three times a week. *The Star*, *Crusader*, *Vanguard*, *The St Lucia Mirror* and *One Caribbean* are weekly publications.

The St Lucia Tourist Board publishes *Tropical Traveller* every two months with listings and features about the island's attractions. The St Lucia Hotel and Restaurant Association produces a bi-annual magazine, *Visions of St Lucia*, which promotes restaurants and provides information about upcoming events and is distributed through the island's hotels. A free biannual magazine, *Paradise St Lucia*, is available across the island.

### TV

There are two television channels, Channel 4 and DBS; St Lucia also receives a host of programmes from the USA via satellite.

### Radio

The island has three radio stations: Radio St Lucia, Radio 100 and Radio Caribbean International, which broadcast a variety of local news and music.

### ELECTRICITY

220 volts, 50 cycles AC and 110 volts, 60 cycles AC.

### FACILITIES FOR THE DISABLED

Facilities for disabled visitors are few, although newer hotels will be better equipped than others. In Castries and elsewhere the curbs and pavements can be high and difficult for wheelchair users and the physically challenged to negotiate. That said, there are still many visitor attractions that are accessible. Check with your travel agent that your hotel has the facilities you need and that the places you want to visit can accommodate you.

> ### Shopping in Castries
> Pointe Seraphine is a modern mall at the cruise ship terminal, with public telephones, an ATM and a cafe. On sale are designer goods and locally made crafts and art at Bagshaws and St Lucia Fine Arts; St Lucia Jazz Festival tickets are available from a booth here. Across the harbour is La Place Carenage precinct. Remember your passport and airline ticket for duty free shopping.
>
> Saturday is market day in the capital and Central Market and the Vendors' Arcade keep a brisk pace. On the outskirts of town is Gablewoods Mall with a pharmacy, book shop, boutiques, gift shops and plenty of places to eat.

### WHAT TO WEAR

Stick to cool and comfortable attire in the heat. Wearing skimpy shorts, skirts or beachwear while sightseeing and shopping in town is considered inappropriate. Most restaurants prefer their guests to dress elegantly casual, however some of the more upmarket establishments may require men to wear a jacket and a tie.

In winter the evenings can be cool, so it would be wise to carry a light cardigan or wrap; don't forget to take a lightweight umbrella or raincoat to protect you from brief showers during the rainy season.

### EMERGENCIES

Police **999**
Fire and Ambulance **911**
The main police station is located on Bridge Street, Castries.

### MEDICAL SERVICES

The main public medical facility on the island is the large Victoria Hospital in Castries (tel: 453 7059), which has a 24-hour emergency department. Private hospitals include St Jude's Hospital in Vieux Fort (tel: 454 6041), which has an emergency department

### Getting Married in St Lucia

An increasing number of couples choose to tie the knot while on holiday in St Lucia. That way they can combine the wedding and honeymoon, and even bring friends and relations along too.

Couples can opt to have their nuptials barefoot on the beach, in a small island church, or at a national landmark, such as Diamond Botanical Gardens, Pigeon Island National Landmark or at the foot of the Pitons.

Tour operators in the UK and USA offer all-inclusive wedding and honeymoon packages, while larger hotels have a dedicated wedding planner, who can arrange every detail, whether it's a simple ceremony or a lavish family affair.

Before the wedding couples will need to be resident on St Lucia for four days. However, after two days a local lawyer can begin the process and apply for a licence on the couple's behalf – It needs to be applied for at least two working days before the ceremony.

Documents required before the wedding can take place are:
• A valid passport
• Birth certificate
• Divorcees should bring their Decree Absolute
• Widows/widowers should bring the death certificate of their spouse and also their original marriage certificate
• A deed pool is required if there has been a name change
• If the bride or groom is under 18 the parents must provide their consent in a sworn affidavit stamped by a Notary Public

Tips for a troublefree tropical wedding:
• Choose your wedding outfit carefully, the heat can play havoc with your hair and clothing.
• Check that the airline can transport the wedding clothes safely, either boxed or in a protective garment bag. Also contact the hotel in advance regarding pressing delicate fabrics.
• Choose your photographer wisely, photographs and a video of the event could be your only mementoes.

as well, and the small Taipon Hospital in the south of Castries (tel: 459 2000). Elsewhere there are medical centres and clinics in Soufrière (tel: 459 7258/5001) and Dennery (tel: 453 3310).

## DEPARTURE TAX

All visitors are required to pay a departure tax of EC$54, however this is usually included in the ticket price.

## SECURITY AND CRIME

St Lucia is a relatively safe island but crime, especially petty theft, certainly exists. By all means relax while on holiday but don't leave home without your common sense. Keep an eye on personal possessions and important documents when wandering in the markets and the busy resort areas; keep your money in a safe place, and leave your expensive jewellery at home or in the hotel safe. If you are renting a car keep valuables out of sight, preferably locked in the boot; don't offer lifts to strangers. Avoid the beaches and out of the way side streets after dark.

It is likely that you will be approached by vendors offering anything from hair braiding to crafts and a variety of souvenirs on the beach and at tourist attractions. If you are interested in what's on offer then haggle for an agreeable price, but if not don't waste people's time. A firm, but polite "no thank you" is usually sufficient to deter any further advances.

## DIPLOMATIC REPRESENTATION

**British High Commission**, 2nd floor Francis Compton Building, Waterfront, Castries; tel: 452 2484; fax: 453 1543; email: briitishhc@candw.lc
**US Embassy**, located in Barbados, at the Canadian Imperial Bank of Commerce (CIBS) Building, Broad Street, Bridgetown, tel: (246) 436 4950/429 5246.

# ACCOMMODATION

St Lucia has a reputation for expensive all-inclusive accommodation but in fact there is a choice of places to stay, with something for every budget from large, exclusive all-inclusive resorts to small, intimate inns and basic bed and breakfasts. Self-catering apartments and luxury villas are also available to rent.

Basic bed and breakfasts run by St Lucians who open up their homes to visitors are popular with budget-conscious travellers who don't mind staying off the beaten track and don't need the creature comforts offered by the upmarket resorts. One thing to note though is that a few of the small home from homes do not have hot water, so be sure to check when booking if this is important to you.

The beauty of staying with a local family is that you will have the chance to experience first hand the real St Lucia. Local people will also be able to point you in the direction of little-known sights and the best places to enjoy authentic Creole cuisine. If you are staying in a rural area or far from reliable public transportation links you are best advised to rent a sturdy vehicle, or employ a guide because taxi fares can mount up.

The wild side of the island is never far away from the splashy hotels and resorts, in fact most have made a feature of the bays, valleys and forests where they are situated. For years eco-tourists were denied the opportunity to truly get close to nature, to sleep under canvas and enjoy the clear Caribbean starlit sky. That has all changed with the opening of St Lucia's first official campsite at Anse La Liberté, south of Canaries on the West Coast. Tents stand on a raised platform so as to protect campers from unfriendly critters, great fun for lovers of the outdoors, especially so close to the forest and the bays.

Off-season rates (mid-April to mid-December) can be substantially lower than high-season rates (mid-December to mid-April). Be prepared to pay a 10 percent service charge and a government tax of 8 percent, but for all-inclusive package holidays this may already be included in the price you are quoted. Rates are subject to change, so always check in advance.

The price categories quoted below are for a double room a night in high season. European and American meal plans are available. Most resort hotels will provide an all-inclusive price on request, otherwise your travel agent can supply you with a quote.

$$$$ Luxury = above US$500+
$$$ Expensive = US$200–500
$$ Moderate = US$100–200
$ Inexpensive = US$50–100

## CASTRIES

**Auberge Seraphine**, Vigie Cove, Castries, tel: 453 2073; fax: 451 7001; www.aubergeseraphine.com
Small city hotel close to George F.L. Charles Airport and central Castries. Simple accommodation with view of the harbour. Swimming pool and beach shuttle available for guests. $
**Eudovic Guest House**, Goodlands, Castries, tel: 452 2747; fax: 459 0124 Small, friendly guesthouse run by local artist and woodcarver Vincent Eudovic and his family. Ten minutes from Castries centre. Rooms are simple with lovely furniture made from local wood, a kitchenette and fan. The artist's studio is at the same property. $
**Green Parrot Hotel**, Morne Fortune, tel: 452 3399/452 3167; fax: 453 2272 Large, comfortable rooms in a well-

established hotel, with good views over Castries. The hotel has a popular and well-known restaurant. **$**

**Orange Grove Hotel**, Bois d'Orange, tel: 452 0021; fax: 452 8094; www.orangegrovehotel.com

Small intimate hill property near Castries. with large, brightly decorated rooms. Swimming pool on site and guests can make use of the shuttle service to Waves at Choc Beach. **$–$$**

**Rendezvous Resort**, Malabar Beach, tel: 452 4211; fax: 452 7419; www.romanticholiday.com

Couples-only all-inclusive, medium-sized hotel popular with honeymooners. Set in pretty gardens with friendly staff. Cool beachfront and garden suites, swimming pool, whirlpool and lovely beach. Close to Castries centre and George F. L. Charles airport so some people might be bothered by the planes flying overhead. **$$–$$$$**

**St James's Club Morgan Bay**, Gros Islet, tel: 450 2511; fax: 450 1050; email: res@eliteislandresorts.com; www.eliteislandresorts.com

Large, modern all-inclusive property on Choc Bay with swimming pools, hot tub and water sports facilities. Spacious bedrooms are tastefully decorated and guests have a choice of a sea or garden view. Families are welcome. **$$$–$$$$**

**Sandals Halcyon Beach St Lucia**, Choc Bay, tel: 453 0222; fax 451 8435; www.sandals.com

The smallest of the three Sandals all-inclusive, couples-only resorts. This luxury hotel is a short drive from Castries centre and is set in lovely tropical gardens with a good restaurant on the pier. Rooms are spacious and comfortable. With swimming pools and a good beach. Guests have access to the sister resorts. **$$$$**

**Sandals Regency St Lucia Golf Resort & Spa**, La Toc Road, tel: 452 3081; fax: 452 1012; www.sandals.com

One of three Sandals couples-only hotels. This upmarket all-inclusive resort stands on a hill just outside Castries, near La Toc Battery. Some of the luxurious suites have private plunge pools. There is also a pretty beach, a choice of swimming pools and a nine-hole golf course. **$$$$**

**Top O' the Morne Apartments**, The Morne, tel: 452 3603; fax: 453 1433; email: info@topothemorne.com; www.topothemorne.com

Smart, spacious apartments in a colonial-style building with cool verandas and patios that afford panoramic views over The Morne, Castries, and to Martinique on a clear day. The complex has a swimming pool, tennis court and a shuttle transports guests to the beach. Long term rentals are available and car hire can be arranged. **$–$$**

**Villa Beach Cottages**, Choc Bay, tel: 450 2884; fax: 450 4529; email: info@villabeachcottages.com; www.villabeachcottages.com

A small collection of self-contained cottages and suites situated on Choc

Bay. Water sports facilities and swimming pool on site. **$$**

## LABRELOTTE BAY

**East Winds Inn**, Labrelotte Bay, tel: 452 8212; fax: 452 9941; email: eastwinds@candw.lc; www.eastwinds.com
Small intimate, all-inclusive beachfront hotel with views of Labrelotte Bay and stylish cottage accommodation. The property is set in lush tropical gardens and has a gourmet restaurant. **$$–$$$**

**Windjammer Landing Resort**, Labrelotte Bay, tel: 456 9000; fax: 452 9454; www.windjammer-landing.com
Large upmarket villa property in the hills with great views over the bay and within sight of Reduit Beach. The exclusive resort has luxurious accommodation and celebrity clientele. Families welcome. Tennis, water sports and swimming pools and spa facilities. **$$–$$$$**

## RODNEY BAY

**Bay Gardens Hotel**, Rodney Bay, tel: 452 8060; fax: 452 8059; email: baygardens@candw.lc; www.baygardenshotel.com
Friendly family hotel with pretty gardens on the south side of Rodney Bay Marina, near to Reduit Beach. Comfortable rooms with a balcony or patio, some with kitchenette; some rooms also have disabled access. Freshwater pools and children's swimming pool. **$$**

**Coco Kreole**, Rodney Bay, tel: 452 0712; fax: 452 0774; email: cocokreole@candw.lc; www.cocokreole.com
Small, trendy boutique hotel near Reduit Beach and the tourist strip's restaurants and bars. A shuttle transports guests to the beach. The simple, comfortable rooms are decorated in bright colours of the Caribbean. **$–$$**

**Harmony Suites**, Rodney Bay, tel: 452 8756; fax: 452 8677; email: harmony@candw.lc; www.harmonysuites.com
Comfortable, moderately priced suite accommodation near Reduit Beach with views of the marina and the countryside; some rooms have kitchenettes, which are suitable for families. **$$**

**Marlin Quay Resort**, Gros Islet, tel: 452 0393; fax: 452 0383; email: marlin@candw.lc; www.marlin-quay.com
Townhouse and suite development on a pretty waterfront. Rooms are airy

*By the pool at LeSport*

and colourfully decorated with plunge pools, freshwater swimming pool and a children's pool area. The complex is near Reduit Beach, with water sports facilities and a choice of restaurants. Within walking distance from Rodney Bay's busy nightlife. **$$–$$$**

**Papillon**, Reduit Beach, Rodney Bay, tel: 452 0984; fax: 452 9332; email: papslu@rexresorts.net; www.rexresorts.com
One of three Rex Resorts on the same hotel complex with comfortable air-conditioned rooms and en suite bathrooms. Swimming pools and water sports facilities. All-inclusive packages available. **$$$**

**Rex St Lucian**, Reduit Beach, Rodney Bay, tel: 452 8351; fax: 452 8331; email: stlsu@rexresorts.net; www.rexresorts.com
One of three Rex Resorts on the same complex this upmarket hotel stands in the heart of Rodney Bay on Reduit Beach, one of the best on the island. Lovely spacious rooms with garden or sea views; air-conditioning and en suite bathroom; three very good restaurants on site. With swimming pools and water sports facilities for guests right on the beach, floodlit tennis courts and a gym. All-inclusive packages available. **$$$**

**Royal St Lucian**, Reduit Beach, Rodney Bay, tel: 452 9999; fax: 452 9639; email: rslslu@rexresorts.net; www.rexresorts.com
The most luxurious of the three Rex Resorts. This all-inclusive resort has deluxe all suite accommodation, four elegant restaurants and water sports facilities on Reduit Beach. **$$$$**

**Tropical Villas**, Reduit Beach, tel: 450 8240/0349; fax: 450 8089; email: tropvil@candw.lc; www.tropicalvillas.net
Luxury villas and townhouses for rent in Rodney Bay, Cap Estate in the far north, Bois d'Orange near Vigie peninsula and on the West Coast in and around Soufrière. Not all of the villas are beachfront properties but most have private swimming pools, and maid service is included in the price. **$$–$$$**

## NORTH COAST

**Club St Lucia by Splash**, Cap Estate, Smugglers Village, tel: 450 0551; fax: 450 0281; email: clubstlucia@splashresorts.com; www.splashresorts.com
Large, splashy all-inclusive resort in Smugglers Village. Luxurious accommodation in spacious cottages with balconies or patios overlooking landscaped grounds, long stretch of beach, five restaurants, several bars and swimming pools. **$$$**

**Glencastle Resort**, Massade, Gros Islet, tel: 450 0833; fax: 450 0837; www.glencastleresort.net
A small hotel situated in the hills north of Rodney Bay. Comfortable, rooms have a balcony and a sea or garden view. Rooftop swimming pool and restaurant on the property. Children welcome. **$**

**Hotel Capri**, Smugglers Cove, Cap Estate, tel: 450 0009; fax: 450 0002; www.capristlucia.com
A small, elegant and intimate inn on Cap Estate in St Lucia's far north, in a picturesque location overlooking the sea. Spacious, tastefully decorated rooms have en suite bathrooms and sea views. Swimming pool and a good restaurant on site. Rent rooms or the rent the whole villa exclusively. **$$$–$$$$**

**LeSport**, Cariblue Beach, tel: 457 7800/450 8551; fax: 450 0368; email: reservations@thebodyholiday.com; www.thebodyholiday.com
A luxury all-inclusive spa resort in the far north of the island set in a hillside with a beautiful palm-shaded beach; suites are spacious and tastefully furnished and there are also lovely rooms for guests travelling alone. The restaurant serves great food and there is live entertainment. Almost everything is

included in the price including alcoholic drinks and many of the spa treatments. $$$$

**Sandals Grande St Lucian Spa & Beach Resort**, Pigeon Island Causeway, Gros Islet, tel: 455 2000; fax: 455 2001; www.sandals.com

One of three Sandals resorts on the island, this couples-only (heterosexual) all-inclusive luxury resort stands next to the Pigeon Island National Landmark. With brightly decorated and spacious rooms, a lovely stretch of golden sand, five swimming pools, a spa and a varied choice of restaurants. $$$$

## MARIGOT BAY

**The Inn On The Bay**, Marigot Bay, tel: 451 4260; email: info@saint-lucia.com

A small adult-only inn set in the hillside overlooking the bay. Rooms have fans and verandas which catch the breezes; some en suite bathrooms have a shower only. $$

**JJ's Paradise Resort**, Marigot Bay, tel: 451 4076; fax: 451 4146; email: jj@jjparadise.com; www.jjparadise.com

A St Lucian-owned and operated resort, popular with the sailing fraternity because of its location close to sheltered Marigot Bay. Good local food available at the restaurant well-known for its seafood. Clean, spacious air-conditioned cottages and bungalows with teak furniture and verandas overlooking the bay. Located at about a 20-minute drive south of Castries and a 55-minute drive north of the Pitons in Soufrière. $$

**Marigot Beach Club Hotel & Dive Resort**, Marigot Bay, tel: 451 4974; fax: 451 4973; email: mbc@candw.lc; www.marigotdiveresort.com

Rooms and villas on the waterfront with great views of the bay out to the Caribbean Sea and the surrounding countryside. A popular place to stay for dive and water sports enthusiasts

> ### ◑° Divers' Paradise
> The warm, clear Caribbean waters that lap the island of St Lucia have made it popular with scuba divers and snorkellers. Several hotels and resorts offer dive holiday packages, which should cover all dive expenses and a stay in a comfortable hotel. Anse Chastanet, Jalousie Hilton, Ti Kaye, Windjammer Landing, The Inn On The Bay, Oasis Marigot and St James's Club have comprehensive packages for divers and other water lovers. For more information contact the St Lucia Tourist Board in your home country or visit: www.stlucia.org

and also the home of Doolittles Restaurant. $$

**Oasis Marigot**, Marigot Bay, tel: 1-800 263 4202 (North America); 00 800 2785 8241 (UK); fax: (305) 946 6372 (US); email: info@oasismarigot.com; www.oasismarigot.com

A large villa complex near to Marigot Marina and yacht moorings. The Oasis group's villas located on the north side of the bay are only accessible by boat. Most of the properties have good views of the bay and the palm-fringed beach. $$–$$$

## SOUFRIERE

**Anse Chastanet Resort**, Soufrière, tel: 459 7000; fax: 459 7700; email: ansechastanet@candw.lc; www.ansechastanet.com

Lovely and spacious, open-sided but private accommodation set in a hillside with breathtaking views. Stylish decoration and furnishings made from local wood and textiles. Popular choice for honeymooners. The resort has a volcanic sand beach (which guests make use of just the same), but nearby Anse Mamin has a stretch of fine white sand. Excellent dive facilities on site run by Dive St Lucia. No disabled access because the suites

**Camping in St Lucia**

Getting back to nature is the reason why ecotourists flock to the island with its pristine coral reefs and lush rainforest that is the habitat of rare birds and wildlife. Visitors can sleep under the stars at St Lucia's only official campsite at Anse La Liberté, which is managed by the St Lucia National Trust. Camping can provide a very different experience to a stay in one of the luxury resorts that pepper the landscape. For the price of a night at a budget hotel or guesthouse campers can rent a tent on a raised platform or on the ground. Call 453 7656 for more information.

can be reached only by a set of steep steps. **$$$–$$$$**

**Hummingbird Beach Resort**, off the Anse Chastanet Road, tel: 459 7232/7492; fax: 459 7033; email: hbr@candw.lc; www.nvo.com/pitonresort; www.istlucia.co.uk

Small hotel on the West Coast just outside Soufrière centre. Most rooms have a view of the sea and the Pitons and easy access to the beach. Cottage with kitchen also available. **$$**

**Jalousie Hilton Resort & Spa**, Jalousie Bay, tel: 459 8000/7666; fax: 459 7667; www.jalousie.hilton.com

Expansive property with luxury villa and suite accommodation on the old Jalousie Plantation. Private plunge pools and swimming pool; beach in a sheltered bay, helipad and spectacular views of the Pitons. All-inclusive packages available. **$$$–$$$$**

**La Dauphine Estate**, Soufrière, tel: 450 2884; fax: 450 4529; email: info@villabeachcottages.com; www.villabeachcottages.com

Cottage and Great House for rent on a 19th-century plantation 8km (5 miles) from Soufrière. Rooms are decorated and furnished in colonial style and there are nature trails and forest close by where guests can hike. **$$**

**La Haut Plantation**, West Coast Road, tel: 459 7008; fax: 459 5975; www.lahaut.com

A pretty, family-run guesthouse in a colonial-style building, with wrap around verandas. The main building was once a cocoa house and La Haut is still a working farm. Simple, airy rooms have en suite bathroom and private balcony. A self-contained cottage is also available to rent. **$$**

**Ladera Resort**, Soufrière tel: 459 7323; fax: 459 5156; email: Ladera@candw.lc; www.ladera-stlucia.com

Upscale and exclusive villa and suite hillside property 3km (2 miles) from the centre of Soufrière. Accommodation crafted from stone and rich hardwood is open on one side, has beautiful furnishings and private plunge pool. Lovely tropical gardens and breathtaking views over Soufrière Bay to the Pitons; excellent cuisine at Dasheene Restaurant. **$$$–$$$$**

**Mago Estate Hotel**, West Coast Road, tel/fax: 459 7352; email: info@magohotel.com; www.magohotel.com

In the hills just above Soufrière, overlooking the Pitons. Accommodation is scattered throughout lush gardens containing tropical fruit trees and hammocks. Rooms have an open side from which to view Soufrière Bay and enjoy the sounds of nature. En suite shower facilities. Plunge pool and a swimming pool. **$$–$$$**

**The Still Plantation and Beach Resort**, Soufrière, tel: 459 5049/ 5179; fax: 459 5091; email: contact@thestillresort.com; www.thestillresort.com

Two hotels under the same umbrella, the beach resort is on Anse Chastanet Road and the plantation accommodation is on Lewis Street. Simple air-conditioned bedrooms with en suite bathrooms and sea views; some have kitchen facilities. Swimming pool and volcanic sand beach, gardens and plantation tours available. **$–$$**

**Stonefield Estate Villa Resort**, Soufrière, tel: 459 7037/5648; fax: 459 5550; www.stonefieldvillas.com

Small villa complex in landscaped gardens almost 2km (1 mile) from Soufrière. Each villa, named after a flower, is individual, some have a garden shower, a veranda and panoramic views of the Pitons, the sea and Soufrière. Swimming pool and good restaurant on the property. **$$–$$$**

**Ti Kaye Village Resort**, tel: 456 8101/2; fax: 456 8105; email: Info@TiKaye.com; www.tikaye.com

West Coast hideaway on a cliffside just outside Soufrière. Accommodation in stylish, Caribbean-style cottages in lush gardens. The beach is a short walk down a set of wooden steps. Good choice for divers since the marine life is plentiful and the *Lesleen M* shipwreck is just offshore. **$$–$$$**

## VIEUX FORT AND THE SOUTH

**Balenbouche Estate**, tel: 455 1244; fax: 455-1342; email: balenbouche@candw.lc; www.balenbouche.com

Family-run guesthouse with colonial-style villas to rent on an old 18th-century sugar plantation that remains a working farm. A popular heritage site with tropical gardens used for weddings and as a St Lucia Jazz Festival venue. Amerindian artifacts have been discovered on the property. **$–$$**

**Skyway Inn**, Beanfield, Vieux Fort, tel: 454 7111/5; fax: 454 7116; email: skyway@slucia.com

Medium-sized, economically-priced modern hotel on a hillside close to Anse de Sables beach, the island's windsurfing centre. Five minutes from the centre of historic Vieux Fort. Simple rooms, some with kitchenette. The inn has a rooftop swimming pool and bar, and runs a shuttle service to Hewanorra International Airport. **$–$$**

## EAST COAST

**Fox Grove Inn**, Mon Repos, Micoud, tel: 455 3271; email: foxgroveinn@candw.lc; www.foxgroveinn.com

Small country hotel close to Mamiku Gardens. Simple guestrooms have en suite showers or bathrooms and ceiling fans. Good views of Praslin Bay. Popular with nature-lovers. **$**

*Sunset at the Jalousie Hilton Resort*

# INDEX